Active PARENTING *now*

For Parents of Children Ages 5 to 12

by Michael H. Popkin, Ph.D.

To my parents, Naomi and Harry Popkin
To the memory of my mother, Mona Rubin Popkin
To my wife and parenting partner, Melody Popkin
And to our children, Megan and Benjamin Popkin

Thank you for the gift of family.

ISBN 1-880283-49-2

Photography by Sonny Senser of Santaguida Photography and Michael H. Popkin
Cover design by Gabrielle Jenkins

Acknowledgements

Active Parenting Now is based on the time-tested theories of some of the great psychologists of the twentieth century. Chief among them are two Austrian psychiatrists who, though now deceased, continue to exert a profound influence on how we can effectively parent our children. Their names are Alfred Adler and Rudolf Dreikurs. I respectfully acknowledge that their contributions lie at the heart of this program.

Complementing the theories of Adler and Driekurs, I have included communication skills that have grown out of the pioneering work of Carl Rogers, Robert Carkhuff, and Thomas Gordon. I am also indebted to the work of Haim Ginott, Albert Ellis, and Milton Erickson.

I also acknowledge and thank my two mentors, Professor Kenneth Matheny of Georgia State University and Professor Oscar Christensen of the University of Arizona. You are much more a part of this program than the one story that I "borrowed" from each of you. Thanks are also expressed to Professor Roy Kern of Georgia State University, who first introduced me to parenting education some 30 years ago, and to Frank Walton, who just keeps on encouraging.

Finally, I would like to acknowledge the tremendous work of the staff at Active Parenting Publishers, who continue to make the dream of Active Parenting a daily reality. A special thank you to Rachel Metzger, Director of Product Development, and her team, Carol Keller, Jessica Schelly, and Marcella O'Steen, who saw this project through to completion. And to a very special employee of the company, my father, Harry G. Popkin—social worker, camp director, role model, and inspiration. It's been great working with you, Dad.

Michael H. Popkin
Atlanta, Georiga

Table of Contents

Preface

Active Parenting Publishers, founded in 1980, created the world's first video-based parenting education program. The need for such an innovation in parenting education was based on two beliefs about parenting in our modern democratic society:

1. Parenting well is extremely important.

2. Parenting well is extremely difficult.

It is also assumed that most parents want to parent well, but have not been given the necessary skills or support.

This lack of training can be disastrous in our modern society, where children openly reject traditional parenting methods. Everywhere, we find parents and children engaging in frustrating struggles for power. Families often become an energy drain and source of frustration rather than a support network and source of satisfaction. Worse, many children are not developing the basic qualities of character necessary for thriving in our modern society: courage, responsibility, cooperation, respect and self-esteem.

Consequently, many parents of young children express fear about the choices their children will make when they become teenagers. This fear may be well founded. Teenage drug use, pregnancy, abortion, crime, AIDS, and suicide all remain at frighteningly high levels.

Obviously, parenting is not the only influence on a child's development, but it is the one we can do the most about. This Parent's Guide has been designed to teach you a method of parenting and problem solving that will help you prepare your children to courageously meet the challenges life will pose. And it will help you build relationships that bring joy and satisfaction for a lifetime.

At the end of our lives, we will not remember how much money we made, how many ball games we watched, or how many things we possessed. What will come back to us in a brilliant and blinding light is the quality of the relationships we formed with those we loved: our friends, our spouses, our children.

Perhaps the truest thing that can be said about parenting is that it requires a lot of energy. It is a tremendously "active" undertaking, requiring a 24/7 commitment with a myriad of skills ranging from discipline to communication and support. Children, it seems, respond better to actions than to words. And so, to be an effective parent is to be an active parent. This is one of the reasons we have chosen the name *Active Parenting Now* for this course.

We also think of the word "active" as a contrast to the "reactive" approach used by most parents. Reactive parents wait until their children push them to their limits, then they react. Often they react with frustration, anger, and random discipline ... or as one mother put it, "the screech and hit" school of parenting. When parents "react" rather than "act," they are allowing the child to control both the situation and the parent's own emotions. Problems tend to continue or even get worse as parent and child re-act the same frustrating scenes over and over.

Our philosophy in Active Parenting Now is that it is the job of the parent, rather than the child, to play the leadership role in the family.

Part of the problem is that most parents do not have a consistent approach to parenting. They use a little of what their parents did, a little of the exact opposite of what their parents did, and a little of what they picked up from friends, books, and magazine articles. Our philosophy in *Active Parenting* Now is that it is the job of the parent, rather than the child, to play the leadership role in the family. This course will help you clarify your own goals for your child and teach you effective methods for leading your child toward them. But it will do more. It will also teach you a consistent model of parenting, enabling you to act with confidence and clarity as you encounter the many challenges parents face.

There are other reasons we chose to emphasize the word "active." This is an age of active people, who are engaged in a host of active pursuits: jobs and careers, community work, political causes, the arts, hobbies, and sports. The fact that you are reading this book shows that you are one of these active people; you are taking steps toward improving your family interactions, and you are seeking information to help you excel as a parent. So *Active Parenting Now* is for active people like you.

This program is also "active" in another sense. It uses learning methods that call for the active involvement of all participants. Active learning is effective learning, and we believe we have developed a parenting program that uses the most effective learning approaches available. First, *Active Parenting Now* uses the combined power of video presentations and group interactions (either in the classroom setting or over the internet). We think you will find that you can become actively involved in such a process — that you can absorb information, sharpen your insights, hone your ideas, and share them with others in a process that will become dynamic for you. Second, we have fun with group learning exercises in which every participant can take an active role. And third, we make use of this Parent's Guide.

This Parent's Guide is a resource providing you with useful information and practical skills. Most parents find it helpful to review key concepts in it from time to time. The Parent's Guide also contains activities for use at home and in your group. These activities will strengthen your ability to use the skills of *Active Parenting Now* and are an important part of your learning experience.

A word of caution: During the next six weeks, you will learn a very practical model for understanding and leading children. This model has been used effectively by millions of parents, counselors, teachers and psychologists. It works! However, it is put into use by human beings, and human beings, as we all know, are imperfect. We make mistakes. During this workshop you will probably become aware of two kinds of mistakes of your own:

First, you may realize or recall mistakes you have made in the past in your own parenting. Almost everyone does. It is important that you recognize these mistakes, but it is much more important that you let them go. They are in the past, and it is useless to dwell on them now. It's much more productive to concentrate on being a more effective parent in the present and in the future!

Second, you will make further mistakes as you learn these new skills. Mistakes are part of the learning process, and they happen to everyone using new skills. So it is important that you accept your mistakes without punishing yourself for being imperfect. If you are too hard on yourself, you not only make yourself feel bad, you also put limits on your learning. This is because when we feel criticized, even by ourselves, we become defensive. Soon we don't even admit our mistakes to ourselves, and we lose the valuable opportunity to correct and improve our performance. Mistakes are for learning; please be gentle with yourself!

Parenting: The Most Important Job

If the future of our society is our children, then the key to that future rests primarily with parents and teachers.

Parenting, though still one of the most underrated jobs in our society, is beginning to attract some of the attention and consideration it deserves. After all, if the future of our society is our children, then the key to that future rests primarily with parents and teachers. Many schools, religious institutions, mental health centers, and other community organizations are responding to this reality by offering support to parents through programs such as *Active Parenting Now.*

The Purpose of Parenting

Success at any job first requires a sound understanding of its purpose. The basic purpose of parenting has not changed throughout history. We can state it like this:

The purpose of parenting is to protect and prepare our children to survive and thrive in the kind of society in which they live.

Although this purpose has not changed over the years, our society has changed in the following ways:

It is more dangerous. The illegal drugs available to today's children and teens are easier to find and more harmful than ever. Crimes against children — and crimes by children — are more numerous than when we were growing up. There is a serious problem with violence in schools and the risk of terrorism is something we are all concerned about. Even sex can now be life threatening.

This poses a difficult problem for parents. Part of our purpose as parents is to protect our children so they will survive. Yet if we overprotect them, we are not preparing them to survive and thrive on their own. Keep in mind that the job of parenting is to work yourself out of a job! That means preparing your child for independence. Three things will help you do this:

1. **Talk with other adults to get an idea of what risks are reasonable for your child to take in your community.** For example, how old should they be to be left home alone and where is it safe for them to play?

2. **Join with other associations, parent support groups, or other organizations.** Work within your community to make it a better place to rear children.

3. **Allow your child to develop independence gradually.** *Active Parenting Now* will help you learn the skills that will encourage your child to build independence. Because children develop through various stages, appropriate behavior at one age may not be appropriate at another. There

are many good books available to help you know what to expect at these ages and stages of development. Talking with your child's teachers and other parents will help you, too.

Society is more diverse and more just. If the bad news about modern society is that it has become more dangerous, the good news is that it has also become more just. We can be proud that our country was founded on the principle that all people are created equal. In fact, this concept of equality is a hallmark of democratic societies throughout the world.

Today's children do not want to be "seen and not heard" or otherwise treated disrespectfully.*

Unfortunately, the word "all" in the United States of America in 1776 really meant all white males who owned land. The rest were not even allowed to vote. But the ball of social progress was moving, and during the next 150 years such milestones as the end of slavery, the beginning of the Labor movement, and the right of women to vote showed that we intended to fulfill the promise of democracy. Then, in the 1950s with the advent of television, the movement for social equality took a giant leap forward. When Martin Luther King, Jr. spoke of his dream of equality for all humankind, the ever-present eye of the cameras carried his message throughout the world. One group after another — African-Americans, Native Americans, Hispanics, Asians, students, women — began to demand that they, too, be treated as equals. Today, no group wants to be treated as inferior, to unquestioningly do what they are told, to speak only when spoken to, or to otherwise allow themselves to be treated disrespectfully.

The atmosphere of equality in which our children live has created a new challenge for today's active parents. We must now contend with a generation of children who are no longer comfortable with their traditional role of inferiority in society. Today's children do not want to be "seen and not heard" or otherwise treated disrespectfully.*

*Note: Because Active Parenting Now was first published in the United States, historical references refer to this democratic society. Because each democratic society has its own story to tell, parents in countries other than the U.S. may wish to share ways in which their own struggle for equality was achieved.

The methods taught in this book take into account the need for new approaches to leadership in a society of equals. However, the concept that "all (people) are created equal" does not mean that all people are created the same. Differences between people range from the obvious, such as how we look, to the subtle, such as our dreams and values. People also have different roles they play and different responsibilities depending on those roles.

The parent's role is that of a leader, while the child more often plays the role of the learner.

In spite of these differences, we are each considered of equal value and worth under our Constitution. This means we are entitled to equal protection under the law; equal opportunity for employment; an equal right to make our opinions known; and an equal right to be treated respectfully, to name a few.

Likewise, in a family parents and children are equal in some ways and different in others. One big way that parents and children are still different is in the roles they play. The parent's role is that of a leader, while the child more often plays the role of the learner. As the leaders in the family, parents have certain rights and responsibilities that differ from those of their children. For example, we have the responsibility of providing food, clothing, shelter, and protection for our children. We also have the right to drive, vote, use alcohol, and other privileges that are not available to children.

We have the authority to decide many of the matters that affect the lives of our children including matters of health, safety, and family values.

In addition, we have the authority to decide many of the matters that affect the lives of our children including matters of health, safety, and family values. Since this includes how we decide to parent, we will look at the concept of authority more closely later in the chapter.

Society changes at an increasing rate. Today's high-tech society changes faster than any in history. Jobs, even industries, that thrive in one decade may be gone the next, replaced by new technologies that were undiscovered when we were in school. Success in such a high-change society requires children to do much more than just learn. They must also learn how to adapt to change and keep learning. Neither blind obedience nor an attitude of complacency is likely to provide them with the skills and character necessary to navigate the current of change that is likely to come. This course will help you learn methods for empowering your children to be decision makers, problem solvers, team players, and lifelong learners—regardless of what career paths they may choose.

Changes in family make up. Change in society has also affected the very make-up of families. The traditional family of two biological parents and children is no longer the norm. More than half of all children will find themselves in single-parent families or families blended together with parents and children from previous marriages. Many other children will live with grandparents, homosexual parents, or other caregivers with whom they share no previous ties at all. No matter what type of family you are a part of, the skills in this book will help you develop the kind of relationship you and your child need to thrive now and later. Of course, there are other issues that we will not address that are specific to your situation, and we encourage you to check the resource section in the back of the book for more information that can help.

The Risks: Drugs, Sexuality, and Violence

The risks associated with drugs, sexuality, and violence are greatest during the teen years. However, what you do now as parents will make a huge difference in what your children will do later when you are not around. We will focus on four major ways to help you reduce the risk that your children will become harmfully involved in these three areas:

1. Build character and develop skills in your child.

Using the active parenting skills taught in this program will help build five important qualities of character—courage, self-esteem, responsibility, cooperation, and respect.

Using the active parenting skills taught in this program will help build five important qualities of character—courage, self-esteem, responsibility, cooperation, and respect. This guide focuses on ways you can instill these characteristics, and many others, in your child. It also helps you develop the personal skills in your children that they will need to succeed—including problem solving, communication, anger management, and academic success. By developing these characteristics and personal skills we give our children a strong foundation from which to resist easy answers to life's problems, answers such as tobacco, alcohol and other drugs, reckless sexuality, and violence.

In fact, research supports this. The Search Institute has identified a list of 40 Developmental Assets that are key to preventing negative outcomes in child and youth development. These internal assets include commitments, values, competencies, and self-perceptions that, if nurtured within young people, provide them with "internal compasses" to guide their behaviors and choices. (We will take a look at these assets in Chapter 5, but if you want to take a sneak peek at them, see the chart on page 142.)

We believe that parents play a very important role in developing these assets in children, and the skills you'll learn in this guide will help you.

2. Build a strong relationship with our kids.

Our ability to influence the values our children will form and the decisions they will make is to a large extent dependent on the quality of

our relationship with them. If our relationship is mostly negative, kids often reject even our good ideas. They are quick to rebel to show us that we can't push them around. Sometimes this rebellion takes the form of drugs, sexuality, and violence as they intentionally reject our values in these matters. The active model of parenting that we will be learning minimizes this risk while still empowering you to be the leader in the family. The methods taught throughout Active Parenting Now are specifically aimed at building a strong parent-child relationship from which your influence can be effective.

3. Talk persuasively about the risks.

Once you have established a positive relationship with your child, it is important to talk about the specific risks involved with drugs, sexuality, and violence. You want to be as persuasive as possible in making your case and winning over their attitudes, because these are areas in which they will ultimately decide what to do. Discipline can be helpful, but discipline alone is not enough to win the battle for their minds. We will discuss effective communication skills in Chapter Two and address the particular issues involved with drugs, sexuality, and violence in Chapter Six.

The more you can enrich your relationship with your child, the more he will allow you to be an influence in his life.

4. Filtering out negative influences in your child's life.

You can't always be with your children every minute of the day, but that doesn't mean you can't be a major influence in their everyday lives. The Center for Substance Abuse Prevention (CSAP) has identified certain risk factors that our children face in today's society and corresponding protective factors that we can provide and develop to counteract them.   (See the chart on page 184.)

In Chapter Six, we will see some practical ways that you can act as a "filter" to screen out many of these risk factors across the six domains, while also encouraging the positive influences by developing protective factors for your child.

Your Child's Character

Because you will not always be there to ensure that your child makes good decisions, it is important that he develop an underlying framework of beliefs, attitudes, and values that will help him steer a successful course on his own. This is commonly referred to as "character," and it is one of the most important concepts in parenting. Although there are many qualities of character that you will want to instill in your children (like the 40 Developmental Assets we mentioned before), we think there are five that are especially critical for success in today's high-tech, diverse, and democratic society:

A child's courage enables the child to try, fail, and try again, until she masters the challenges life presents.

Courage is the first. Alfred Adler once said that if he could give one gift to a child, it would be courage. If a child is courageous, he reasoned, that child can learn everything else she needs to learn. Coupled with parental guidance, a child's courage enables the child to try, fail, and try again, until she masters the challenges life presents. With too little courage, the child gives up easily or does not try at all. Fear leads to failure, and failure reinforces fear. Such a cycle of discouragement supports a lifelong attitude of regret and resentment. Courage is a foundation upon which the child constructs her personality. It is at the heart of human potential. In this course we consider courage to be so essential to the child's development that we devote much of the fifth chapter to methods of encouraging children, and we will be referring to courage again and again.

Self-esteem is the second quality necessary for thriving in a democratic society. Simply stated, self-esteem is the opinion we have of ourselves. When a child's self-esteem is high, he sees himself as a capable human being who has a good opportunity to succeed at challenges. He also knows that even failure is nothing more than an opportunity for learning, so when he doesn't succeed at first, he does not give up. This perception of himself as a winner gives the child the courage to tackle life's problems through positive behavior, and to take advantage of the wonderful opportunities available in a democratic society. We will explore the critical connection between self-esteem, courage, and behavior in Chapter Five.

A sense of **responsibility** is the third quality a child needs to thrive. Democracy demands that its members make decisions and accept responsibility for the consequences of those decisions. Without individual responsibility, our cherished freedoms will give way to governmental responsibility, where the state will make decisions for us.

Democracy demands that its members make decisions and accept responsibility for the consequences of those decisions.

With freedom and choice comes the responsibility for the consequences of those choices. The reality of our society is that its children will be called upon to make thousands of choices, and they will be held responsible for their choices by experiencing the consequences that follow. Some of these choices will be life and death matters. They will be offered drugs; will they choose to accept? They will face choices about drinking, sex, crime, dropping out, and even suicide. And their parents won't always be there to tell them what to do. But if they have been prepared to make responsible decisions, and have developed the courage to stand behind these decisions, they will be prepared to meet these challenges. We will explore methods designed to teach responsibility to children throughout the program and especially in Chapter Three.

Cooperation is the fourth essential quality children need to develop in order to thrive. In some circles a great deal of emphasis has been placed on competition as the road to success. In reality it has always been those individuals who have been aware of the magic of teamwork who have moved society forward. Helping a child learn that life is neither dependent nor independent, but rather an interdependent experience, is a cornerstone of Active Parenting Now. In a society of equals, cooperation skills have high value, and the child who can cooperate is far more likely to survive and thrive than one who has never learned how. Ideally, the relationship of child and parent is one of cooperation rather than conflict. But cooperation from the child cannot be demanded; it must be won. In each session we will focus on a particular method of achieving cooperative relationships between parent and child through Family Enrichment Activities. In addition, Chapter Two is devoted to teaching ways of winning cooperation through effective communication skills.

Cooperation from the child cannot be demanded; it must be won.

Respect is the fifth quality that we will address, and we will do so in this opening chapter, because it is the cornerstone of life in a democratic society. Teaching our children to respect themselves and others begins at home, but it pays dividends in every area in which they will become involved. Respect is about appreciating the worthwhile qualities in ourselves and others and demonstrating this through actions as well as attitude.

Styles of Parenting

Our goal as parents, then, is to instill in our children the skills and character that will enable them to survive and thrive in our fast changing, diverse, democratic society. This is our responsibility and we have the authority to get the job done. After all, even in a society of equals, authorities still exist. The president of a corporation, the police officer on the street, and the principal in the school are examples of people who have the authority to make final decisions in their domains—and the responsibility to enforce those decisions. They are the leaders. However, there's not much use being a leader if no one is willing to follow you. Here, then, is an important principle of leadership:

Leaders get their ultimate authority from those they lead.

The same is true for parents. We are the authorities in our families. But to be effective, we must have the cooperation of our children. Let's look at three types of leadership and how effective each is likely to be in our current society.

1. Autocratic Style: The Dictator

A **dictator** is one who has absolute control, and the autocratic parent is all-powerful in dictating the lives of his or her children. This parent is a dominating figure who rewards and punishes to enforce his orders. Children are told what to do, how to do it, and when to do it. There is little or no room for them to question, challenge or disagree. The dictator method of parenting worked reasonably well in times when inequality was normal between people, but it works poorly in today's time of equality.

Children who grow up in autocratic families seldom thrive. They either have their spirits broken and give up, or, more often, they rebel. This rebellion usually happens during the teen years, because the child has developed enough power to fight back. The dictator has been the typical parenting style for so many generations that teenage rebellion has come to be accepted by many experts as "normal." This is a mistake. Teenagers do not have to rebel to become independent.

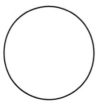

The dictator can be described as using **"limits without freedom."** This style can be depicted as a closed circle.

To his credit, the dictator does understand the need children have for limits. He has the emotional strength and willingness to get involved and to stand firm. But he often goes too far.

You are tending toward the autocratic style of parenting when you say things like:

> *"Because I'm the parent and I said so!"*
> *"As long as you live under my roof, you'll obey my rules."*
> *"When you are the parent, you can decide what to do."*

and when you do things like:

- *tell your teen what to wear*
- *find yourself angry and yelling often*
- *often ground or punish your teen in other ways.*

2. Permissive Style: The Doormat

Permissive parents are often those who are reacting strongly against the harsh and uncompromising autocratic method. Permissive parents allow their children to "do their own thing" too much of the time. In such households, there is little respect for order and routine, and few limits are placed on anyone's freedom. Many such parents behave like doormats, allowing their children to walk all over them. Some of these parents want to be firmer but do not know the words or discipline skills to use. One of the main drawbacks of this style is the feeling of insecurity which plagues children reared this way. They have almost no sense of belonging, and because they have not learned to cooperate, they are often difficult to live with.

Children with permissive parents are often pampered and accustomed to getting their own way. When someone outside the family finally tells them that rules apply to them also, these children or teens frequently rebel. It is difficult to get a child who is used to a lifestyle with no limits to voluntarily begin obeying rules.

 The doormat approach can be described as **"freedom without limits,"** and can be shown as a squiggle line, representing freedom run rampant.

Although the permissive parent's desire to share power with their children and allow them freedom of choice is a good thing, they often go too far.

You are tending towards the permissive style of parenting when you say things like:

> *"I don't think that's a good idea…but, well…okay, if you really want to."*
> *"Do you really need this? Oh, all right. Here's the money."*
>
> *"I sure wish you'd help out around here."*

And when you do things like:

- allow her to go to bed whenever she feels like it

- routinely do his homework with him or go to school to intervene for him often

- give in to her unreasonable demands because you're afraid she will become angry or sad

3. Authoritative Style: The Active Parent

The **authoritative** style is, in some respects, the middle ground between the autocratic and permissive styles, but it is also much more. In an active household, freedom is an ideal, but so are the rights of others and the responsibilities of all. The parent is the leader who encourages cooperation and stimulates learning. There is order and routine, and every person is an important member of the family.

The active parent acknowledges our democratic heritage and the role of social equality among all human beings in two important ways:

1. Children are treated with dignity and respect, even when their parents discipline them.

2. Children are entitled to respectfully express their thoughts and feelings to their parents. In this way they are given the right to influence the decisions that affect their lives. This is consistent with life in a democratic society:

Democracy does not mean you will always get your way.
It means you will always get your say.

The authoritative style can be called **"freedom within limits,"** and can be symbolized by a squiggly line within the limits of a circle.

In fact, it could be shown as "freedom within expanding limits." As the child assumes more and more responsibility, the parent gradually expands the limits, until eventually a teenager leaving home has the same amount of independence as you or I do.

You are tending toward the active style of parenting when you say things like:

"I know you're disappointed, but you can't go. Here's why…"

"Sure we can talk about it. What's your idea?"

"I know you can handle it. But if you need some help, just let me know."

…and when you do things like:

- *involve your child in deciding who will do which family chores*
- *give her the full responsibility for her homework, monitoring her just a little*
- *show an active interest in her education by discussing her subjects with her regularly and attending school functions*
- *involve her in the discipline process by talking with her about your expectations and the consequences for breaking agreements*
- *letting him know what you like about him and encouraging him often*
- *talking with him about topics—such as drug use, sexuality, and violence— in a calm and non-judgmental manner.*

The Method of Choice

A child will resist a parent who robs her of a chance to share in the decisions that affect her life.

One of the single most powerful forces in existence is that of human choice. This concept is so powerful that nations will go to war to preserve their right to choose how to live their lives. When we say that the hallmark of the active style of parenting is "freedom within limits," what we are really talking about is the freedom of the child to make choices.

Just as a people will rise up and overthrow a dictator, a child will resist a parent who robs her of a chance to share in the decisions that affect her life. The parent who is neither a dictator nor a doormat, but an active leader in the family, will use this knowledge to handle problems and teach responsibility.

The freedom to choose is tremendously empowering to children.

Choice is power. As the leader of your family, you can give your child choices that are appropriate for his age and level of responsibility. This, again, is the idea of freedom within expanding limits. The freedom to choose is tremendously empowering to children. And because you exercise your authority to limit what choices the child is allowed to make, family rules and values are not sacrificed.

Don't Boss. Give a Choice.

Even young children can be given simple choices. Allowing your child the opportunity to practice decision making can become a regular part of your daily routine. This can also be useful in helping resolve conflicts as we saw on the video in the example between Katy and Austin. After unsuccessfully trying to coerce Austin into wearing his white shirt, Katy gives Austin a choice.

> *Katy: Would you rather wear this white shirt or the blue one?*
>
> *Austin: The blue one.*

This gives Austin some power over the decisions that affect his life, so he has less need to rebel. He chooses the blue one, which is acceptable to Katy. Had he chosen a shirt that was unacceptable for the situation, Katy would have limited his choice.

Katy: I'm sorry, Austin, the T-shirt with spaghetti stains just isn't appropriate for going out. Let's stick with these two…this white one, or this blue one.

As children get older, the choices they are given can become more open-ended. So instead of either the blue or white shirt, you might simply ask the child what he would like to wear. The following are some examples of choices you can use.

Give Children Choices

Ages 4-7	Ages 8-12
"Would you like orange juice or grapefruit juice this morning?"	"Would you like to help me do the grocery shopping and help choose what we buy?"
"Can you put this away yourself, or would you like some help?"	"Do you prefer to set homework time for before dinner or afterwards?"
"Would you like to pick out a book or would you like me to choose a book for your bedtime story?"	"Would you rather go visit Grandma on Saturday or Sunday?"
"Would you like to take your bath now or after one more song?"	"Which chores would you like to do?"

A word of caution: Don't get carried away and make everything a choice. One parent gave her daughter so many choices that she had to choose from over a dozen different toothbrushes just to brush her teeth at night! No wonder it took forever to get to bed. Sometimes children want and need a firm but friendly decision from a parent. At other times, a limited set of choices is appreciated.

Mutual Respect

Our children are growing up in a society in which people are very sensitive to signs of disrespect. In fact, to disrespect somebody is often considered a personal affront, one that can even lead to violence.

Likewise, learning to respect oneself regardless of strengths, weaknesses, family, culture, or heritage is a building block for self-esteem and success. When we show our children respect, even when we are angry or providing discipline, we help them learn to respect themselves while demonstrating how to treat others respectfully.

Treating our children respectfully is also a good way to teach them how to treat us respectfully.

Treating our children respectfully is also a good way to teach them how to treat us respectfully. As the author, Bernard Malamud once wrote, "respect is what you have to have in order to get." In other words, if we want someone to treat us respectfully, even our children, then we have to be willing to treat them respectfully, too. This concept of "mutual respect," as Rudolf Dreikurs called it, is often easier said than done. Showing children respect means not yelling, cursing, calling them names, being sarcastic, or otherwise speaking to them in ways you would not want them speaking to you. There are also countless more subtle forms of disrespect to guard against. For example, an overprotective parent who is quick to jump in to solve a child's problem—without giving her a chance to struggle to find a solution for herself—is being disrespectful. A parent who always insists on doing what he wants and never compromising to do what the child wants is also showing disrespect.

When we catch ourselves treating our child disrespectfully, it is wise to smile, apologize, and if appropriate, make amends.

Examples:

> *"I'm sorry I yelled at you. That wasn't very respectful. Let me try again more calmly to tell you why I was angry."*
>
> *"I apologize for not calling to tell you I would be late. That wasn't respectful. How can I make it up to you?"*

Teaching our children to show respect to others begins with insisting on their showing us respect. This requires teaching on our part, as well as the use of the discipline skills we will be learning in Chapter Three. The parent who has been careful to show her child respect all along is on solid ground when it comes to correcting the child's disrespectful behavior.

Examples:

> *"I don't talk to you that way. Please do not talk to me that way."*
>
> *"I don't talk to you that way and I will not allow you to talk to me that way."*
>
> *"I want the two of you to stop right now. We don't talk to each other that way in our family."*

Teaching our children to show respect to others begins with insisting on their showing us respect.

As we will see in Chapter Three, when our words alone are not enough to correct misbehavior, we want to use "the method of choice" combined with a logically connected consequence to help get our message through.

Examples:

> *"Either talk to me without yelling or go to your room."*
>
> *"Either share the remote without fighting or there'll be no TV at all."*
>
> *"Either talk to me respectfully about not letting you watch a PG 13 movie or there will be no movies at all this week."*

Finally, the respect with which we treat our spouses, significant others, and even strangers sets an example for our children. When mutual respect is a cornerstone of your own interactions with people, as well as a strong family value, your children come to adopt it almost without trying.

Family Enrichment Activity: Taking Time for Fun

Ever notice that a good salesperson will always spend time developing a positive relationship with you before she tries to sell you anything? She knows that half the job of effectively influencing a person is first developing that relationship. Once the person has been "won over," the sale is much easier. (Can you imagine a salesperson being autocratic and demanding a sale? "You'll buy this because I'm the salesperson and I said so!") The same is true for parenting. The more you can enrich your relationship with your child, the more he will allow you to be an influence in his life. This will prevent many problems as well as make discipline much easier when it is called for.

We will present a Family Enrichment Activity in each chapter. Using these activities, and the other support skills, will strengthen your relationship. If your child is frequently out of control, this may be a way to begin making positive contact. Be creative. Reach out.

The first Family Enrichment Activity is to take time to do something fun with your child. It can be as brief as a few minutes or as long as a day. The key is to make it fun and to try making it a regular part of your relationship. In other words, "Every day a little play." For example:

- *Throw a ball or shoot baskets.*
- *Bake a special dessert together.*
- *Play a game together.*
- *Roughhouse.*
- *Go on an outing ... just the two of you.*
- *Tickle each other.*
- *Tell a joke or funny story.*

To get the most out of this activity:

- *Find activities you both enjoy. Many have little or no cost.*
- *Ask for suggestions from your child, but have some ideas of your own.*
- *Keep it fun! Do not use this time for confrontation.*
- *Record your experiences in your Parent's Guide.*

Family Meetings: Choosing a Family Activity

One of the best ways to prepare your children for success in a democratic society is to teach them the "give and take" that comes with cooperative problem solving or decision making. One excellent way to do this is through Family Meetings. In each chapter of this guide, I'll suggest a different topic for such a meeting. This week I recommend that you hold a brief family meeting to decide what fun activity your family will choose for a family enrichment activity for this week. Keep the meeting informal and brief, so that nobody comes to resent the forum. To keep the meeting running smoothly, start by suggesting one basic ground rule for family meetings, asking if everyone will agree to the following:

We will treat each other respectfully.

Next, ask everyone to contribute some ideas about what that means to them, and list these ideas for future reference. For example:

We will listen while someone else is speaking.

We will wait until the speaker is finished before speaking ourselves.

We will not insult or put down anybody else's ideas.

By getting agreement for these basic ground rules now, you will have the ability to refer to it later whenever someone acts disrespectfully during a meeting. All you need say is, "Remember our agreement to act respect-fully during our meetings?" If this reminder is not enough, you can add the specific violation. For example, "We agreed not to talk when someone else is talking." You may also want to post the ground rules where all family members can review them from time to time.

Be careful, however, not to turn the meeting into one of confrontation. Your goal is to establish family meetings as enjoyable times that allow children to have their voices heard and their wishes considered. Stay upbeat and encouraging as much as possible and you will find that family meetings are a great benefit to parents and children alike.

Taking Care of The Caregiver

We began this chapter by saying that parenting is a very active undertak-ing and that it requires a lot of energy to do well. You might think of this energy as a pitcher of water which you pour out of all day as you take care of the needs of your family, career, volunteer activities, friends, and other demands. By the end of the day this energy can be used up, and your pitcher completely empty.

The idea of taking care of the caregiver (namely you) is that you have to take time each day to restore yourself. While some parents think that taking personal time is selfish, the truth is that you can't do your best if you are constantly overwhelmed, exhausted, burned out, or just plain irritable. Of course, there are parents who go to an extreme in taking care of themselves to the detriment of their children and significant others. But most parents do too little self care and wind up feeling pressured too much of the time. You need to systematically plan (and take!) time away from your children to care for yourself and your other relationships. The following areas can help you plan:

You need to systematically plan (and take!) time away from your children to care for yourself and your other relationships.

Keep your body healthy. Take some time away from your children each day to care for your body. A regular exercise program is great, but a good hot bath can be just the thing at other times, too. Eat a healthy diet, but don't "diet." Keep alcohol and caffeine in moderation. And this is very important: get enough sleep.

Talk and visit with other people. There is an old story about the mother who was at her first dinner party in ages when she noticed that the man sitting next to her was staring at her strangely. Then she realized with horror that while she had been talking to him so intently she had also been cutting his meat for him! Obviously, she needed to get out more. Make sure you take time to talk with friends, spouses, and other adults to keep you connected and recharged.

Clear your mind. Generals used to talk about something called the "haze of battle." It seems that with so much commotion it is sometimes hard to know what is really going on. Parents can find themselves in such a haze, too. To help, take time out when needed—even ten minutes lying on your bed with the door closed can do wonders. Other ways to stay clear is to spend time outdoors, listening to music or reading. Being a life-long learner is also a good way to stay sharp as you develop new interests and skills.

Get organized. A lack of structure and organization is bad for kids and parents alike. When you are constantly worrying about things falling through the cracks and not getting done, you are expending needless energy. Simple time management tools include making and using "to do" lists each day, keeping a family calendar of everyone's activities, and taking time to organize each part of your home.

Decide what you want to do about romance and do it. Not everyone has the same goals about romance in their lives. Some single parents are content to spend time with adult friends and their children, perhaps putting off romance until the kids are grown. Others actively date with or without the intention of marriage. Take some time to think about what is best for you and your family and then actively pursue it. Just be sure that you balance everyone's needs. If you are married or in a significant relationship it is important to take care of your couple relationship. This means going out without the kids at times and taking adult-only vacations. You'd be surprised how the romance can re-bloom when you have a little privacy someplace away from home. And if your marriage needs the help of a counselor, check with your local mental health center, a physician, or other resource for a good referral.

Home Activities

The best way to learn any new skill—from riding a bike, to learning how to use a computer, to new parenting techniques—is to practice, practice, practice. And the more you practice, the more positive the outcome.

Make an effort to put the ideas and skills you are learning to work. The Home Activities will help.

At the end of each chapter, you'll find a list of home activities. These activities are designed to help you practice the ideas and skills presented in the chapter. During the next week, make an effort to put these ideas to work, and record your experiences on the worksheets found at the end of this guide as indicated.

Notice that the last activity for this chapter is to not expect your kids to change this week. It is sometimes easy to forget that it takes years to develop some of the problems that you may experience with your child. Just as it takes a very large ship time to change its course after the rudders are adjusted, it will take time before you begin to see positive changes in the course of your relationship with your child. As you become more familiar with the skills you are learning, these techniques will become more and more natural to you—and you'll begin to see positive changes.

Chapter 1

HOME ACTIVITIES

- Practice giving choices to your child, and complete the worksheet on page 196.

- Find ways to "take care of the caregiver," and begin filling out the chart on page 195.

- Have a Family Meeting about "taking time for fun," and record your results on page 197.

- Don't expect your kids to change this week!

Chapter 2
Winning Cooperation

An oarsman in a Roman galley was rowing to the beat of the drum. He looked over at the oarsman next to him and was horrified at what he saw. The oarsman in the next seat was drilling a hole in the bottom of the boat under his own seat. As the water began to gush into the boat, the first oarsman exclaimed, "What in Jupiter's name are you doing?" The man replied, "What's it to you? I'm only drilling the hole under my seat."

The point of this story, of course, is that when we are all riding in the same boat, no matter whose seat the hole is under, everyone is going to get wet. Nowhere is this more true than in a family. When one member has a problem, the ripples are felt throughout the family.

Active Parenting Now has stressed five main qualities that form the foundation of the individual's ability to succeed in our democratic society: courage, self-esteem, responsibility, and cooperation. Cooperation, the gentle art of working together for the common good, is the subject of this chapter.

The Beauty of Problems

Those who succeed in our society are able to handle problems effectively.

One of the realities of life—whether at home, at work, or in the community—is that problems will arise. This is true for successful people and groups just as it is true for those who are unsuccessful. The difference is that those who succeed in our society are able to handle problems effectively. People who get bogged down in self-pity, play the blame game, make excuses, or make the same mistakes over and over again usually live with fear and anxiety. However, successful people seem to have the courage to cope with problems head on, the self-esteem to believe they will find a solution, the responsibility to accept ownership of the problem, the cooperation and mutual respect to work with others in handling the problem, and the skills necessary to find effective solutions.

Where did they learn all of this? Most likely from dealing with other problems, as children and then as adults, inside the family and out. Problems are a great resource for teaching our children much of what we want them to know. So, when a problem does occur, the active parent will take a deep breath and recognize that, in spite of the inconvenience involved, a wonderful teaching opportunity has just emerged.

To help you take advantage of these opportunities, much of this book is organized around the concept of handling problems. We will begin by looking at ways to build a cooperative relationship with your children. Then we will look at ways you can help them learn how to work with you to solve the problems they own responsibility for handling. In later chapters we will include discipline skills that can help you solve problems of misbehavior with your children. Communication will be a key in both cases as we continue to stress the need for participation and mutual respect in handling problems successfully.

First, let's take a look at the "Problem-Handling Model" to get an overview of how this all fits together.

The Problem-Handling Model

The model for handling problems on the next page includes skills presented in Chapters 2 through 6.

- It begins with preventing many problems through problem-prevention talks *(Chapter 3)* and family talks *(Chapter 6)*.

- When a problem does occur, determine who owns the problem *(Chapter 4)*.

- If the parent owns the problem, or if it is shared, use discipline skills *(Chapter 3)*.

- If the child owns the problem, or if it is shared, use support skills *(Chapter 2)*.

- In any of the three cases, you may decide to refer the problem to a Family Council Meeting *(Chapter 6)*.

- Of course, encouragement is always necessary *(Chapter 5)*.

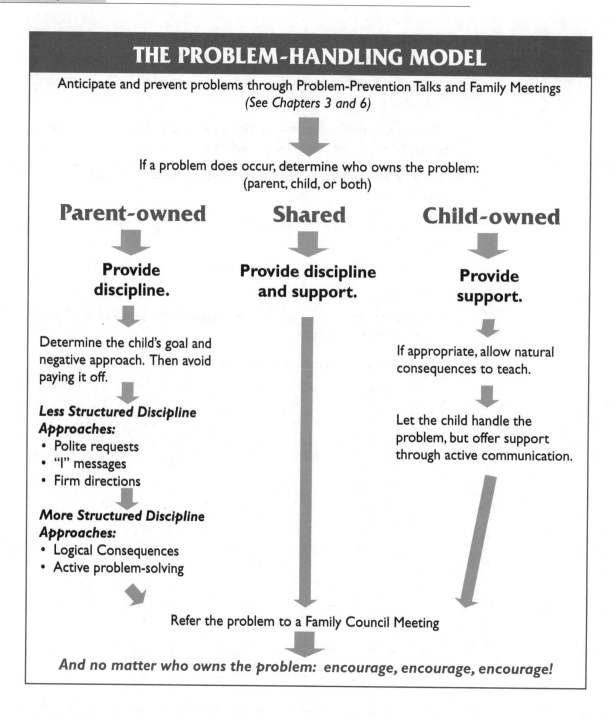

THE PROBLEM-HANDLING MODEL

Anticipate and prevent problems through Problem-Prevention Talks and Family Meetings
(See Chapters 3 and 6)

If a problem does occur, determine who owns the problem:
(parent, child, or both)

Parent-owned

Provide discipline.

Determine the child's goal and negative approach. Then avoid paying it off.

Less Structured Discipline Approaches:
• Polite requests
• "I" messages
• Firm directions

More Structured Discipline Approaches:
• Logical Consequences
• Active problem-solving

Shared

Provide discipline and support.

Child-owned

Provide support.

If appropriate, allow natural consequences to teach.

Let the child handle the problem, but offer support through active communication.

Refer the problem to a Family Council Meeting

And no matter who owns the problem: encourage, encourage, encourage!

Who Owns the Problem?

The first step in handling problems that occur in our families is to determine who owns responsibility for handling the problem. With problems due to children's misbehavior, the parent as leader in the family owns responsibility for finding a solution. The discipline skills on the left side of the Problem-Handling Model can be used to find a solution in these cases. However, there are many problems that children encounter in their lives that are not really our responsibility. These problems are said to be "owned" by the child. When they occur, our job is to offer support using the skills listed on the right side of the model. Sometimes, problems are shared by the parent and the child. In these cases, the parent can offer both support and discipline.

The first step in handling problems that occur in our families is to determine who owns responsibility for handling the problem.

Determining who owns the problem may be a more important part of solving the problem than you might first realize. Children today are very sensitive to their parents trying to run every aspect of their lives. Allowing them the freedom to make decisions, even mistakes, when they own the problem is important in building a cooperative relationship. Dictators take on too many problems as their own. Doormats take on too few. Active parents determine what to do by first determining who owns the problem: themselves or the child. And in some cases they determine that the problem should be shared. In shared situations both discipline and support are often needed.

To help determine who owns a problem, ask yourself the following questions:

? **Who is the problem behavior directly affecting?** Whose needs or goals are being blocked? Who is raising the issue or making the complaint? That person usually owns the problem.

? **Does the problem involve health, safety, or family rules, or values?** If so, then the problem belongs to the parent.

? **Is the problem within reasonable limits for your child's age and level of maturity?** If not, then again, the parent owns responsibility for handling the problem.

Let's look at some examples to help clarify this further.

SITUATION	WHO OWNS the PROBLEM?	Why?
Children are giggling and noisy at a restaurant.	Parent	Parents are eating in a public place and the children's noise is disturbing other patrons and interfering with parents' enjoyment of their meal.
Your child rides her bike on a busy street.	Parent	It is the parents' responsibility to teach their children to use things safely; this situation isn't safe.
Your daughter doesn't like her sister going into her room without asking.	Chld	Siblings are entitled to have a relationship with each other without parents interfering. They need to learn to work out together how they can best get along.
Your child complains that the teacher picks on him.	Child	Children have relationships with other adults. They need to learn how to relate to them on their own.
Your child has a temper tantrum in the supermarket	Parent	The child's behavior is interfering with the parent's goal of shopping.
Your six-year-old complains that he is being picked on by ten-year-olds.	Parent	This would be the child's problem, except that it is beyond his level of maturity to handle.
Your child is not keeping up with his schoolwork.	Shared	The parent's goal of the child being successful in school is blocked, yet school success is also the responsibility of the child.

Notice that last example in the chart is an example of a shared problem. Although schoolwork is the child's responsibility, parents have a right and a responsibility to become involved when the child is not owning this responsibility. The goal in such cases is to shift ownership to the child through both discipline and support methods.

As we move through the next few chapters, we'll learn ways you can support your child when she owns the problem, and also learn effective discipline skills to use when you own the problem. But first, let's talk about an important building block in developing a foundation for either side of the Problem-Handling Model: communication.

Communication: The Road to Cooperation

Many parents have shared that these same communication skills have also made them more effective with coworkers, friends, and even spouses.

Members of a family, like the oarsmen in the Roman galley, are all riding in the same boat. Therefore, teaching our kids how to solve problems cooperatively is in all of our interests, and to do so requires first and foremost, good communication skills. The skills that we will be discussing in this chapter are especially useful in helping our children handle problems that they own. However, over the years, many parents have shared that these same communication skills have also made them more effective with coworkers, friends, and even spouses. Why? Because they help build cooperation, which we define like this:

Cooperation is two of more people working together in a mutually supportive manner for a common goal.

In a high-tech, diverse, democratic society, the child who learns to work cooperatively with others—to be a team player—has a far greater chance at success than the one who overemphasizes competition. Ironically, although the ability to compete is certainly valuable in our society, it is the ability to cooperate that makes both individuals and communities great.

Cooperation is a product of both attitude and skills. We can help our children build a cooperative attitude by first developing one in ourselves. We communicate this attitude through our words and actions by treating our children and others respectfully, enforcing reasonable limits, encouraging participation through family meetings and enrichment activities, and working together to solve problems. Building on this foundation, our next step is to develop the communication skills necessary for working together cooperatively. We may want to win cooperation, but without such skills we find the road filled with mistaken signs—or even blocked. The information and skills in the remainder of this chapter will help you put your good intentions into positive action and pave the road ahead with clear, supportive communication.

Mixed Messages

Communication involves much more than just what you say to your child. In fact, your message is carried on three separate channels:

1 **Your words**

2 **Your tone of voice, and**

3 **Your body language, including hand gestures, how close you stand, and facial expressions.**

When it comes to communicating information like a shopping list, your words carry most of the message. However, with emotionally charged messages such as problems, research has shown that more of the message is carried by body language, followed by tone of voice and lastly, the words themselves. In other words, how you say something is often even more important than what you say.

When all three channels of communication carry the same message, the communication is very clear and powerful. However, when we say one thing with our words and something else with our tone and/or body language, we send a mixed message. Mixed messages not only dilute the strength of the message, but are often confusing to the listener.

For example, imagine that your child owns a problem and you have decided to let her handle it. You say, "I'm not angry. You can do whatever you think is best." However, your tone of voice, crossed arms, and scowl all say, "I'll be angry if you don't do what I think is best." This sort of mixed message makes it difficult for your child to know where she stands. An assertive child will probably hear the message she wants to hear and then do what she wants. Other kids, however, may become anxious and confused about what to do. The key is to adjust your attitude so that you really accept her right to make the decision, even if her choice is not what you would prefer. This will reduce your anger, even if you are still somewhat disappointed. You can also change your words to more honestly reflect your feelings.

Example:

> *"I may be disappointed if you decide not to take your sister with you to the playground, but as I said, it's your choice and I can live with it." (Of course, your face and tone need to communicate this same message.)*

Mixed messages also erode cooperation when the parent owns a problem. For example, you are reading a book when your child asks if he can stay up another hour to watch television. Your words say, "I don't think that's a good idea," but your tone and body language (as you continue to read your book) say, "I'm not really that concerned and if you stay up you probably won't get into trouble."

What do you think your child will do? Like most kids, he will use the confusion to do what he wants to do. Remember, when you split your message you weaken your communication. The clearer you are the more effective you are. Whether using discipline or supporting your child in solving a problem she owns, work to keep your three channels of communication consistent.

Avoiding Communication Blocks

Most parents wish their children would feel freer to come to them with their problems. We want to help them solve these problems and eliminate the pain that such problems can bring. The trouble is that these very problems expose our children's self esteem like a tender nerve. At such times they are hypersensitive to criticism, negative judgment, and other words or actions that seem to say that they are not worthwhile. If we are fortunate enough to engage a child in talking about a problem, we want to first guard against anything that will block communication and prompt her to withdraw.

*A **communication block** is any words, tone of voice or body language that influence a person sharing a problem to end the communication.*

Because you communicate your attitude largely through tone of voice and body language, it is not enough just to watch your words. You have to adopt a supportive, nonjudgmental attitude if you are really going to help. When you listen with an attitude of support, your child will begin to trust you with her feelings and share more of what is going on in her life. This sets the stage for you to influence her to make wise decisions.

If you jump the gun and block communication, you will have lost this valuable opportunity to offer guidance and win cooperation.

Your goal is not to take over and provide a solution, or to take away your child's pain.

Look at the list of common communication blocks on the next page. Each block ignores the child's thoughts and feelings and instead focuses on the parent's attempt to control the situation. More often than not, these attempts backfire. When people are in pain, they want to know that someone else feels their pain with them. The mistake parents make is launching into an attempt to solve the child's problem instead of offering sympathy or encouragement. Ironically, if you try to solve your child's problems, you will actually diminish her self-esteem. Your goal is not to take over and provide a solution, or to take away your child's pain. It is to offer a caring ear, support, and encouragement, and to help your child find a useful solution for herself.

The first step in helping is to identify your most common pitfalls. Once you are aware that you use them, be on guard the next time your child has a problem, and avoid these pitfalls. When you find yourself using them in the future, catch yourself with a smile—and make a change.

BLOCK	EXAMPLE	PARENT'S INTENTION	WHAT IT REALLY SAYS TO THE CHILD
Commanding	"What you should do is..." "Stop complaining!"	To control the situation. To provide quick solutions.	"You don't have the right to decide how to handle your own problems."
Giving Advice	"I've got a really good idea..." "Why don't you..."	To solve the problem for the child.	"You don't have the good sense to come up with your own solutions."
Placating	"It isn't as bad as it seems" "Everything will be okay."	To take away the child's pain; to make him feel better.	"You don't have a right to your feelings. You can't handle discomfort."
Interrogating	"What did you do to make him..."	To get to the bottom of the problem and find out what the child did wrong.	"You must have messed up somewhere."
Distracting	"Let's not worry about that."	To protect the child from the problem by changing the subject.	"I don't think you can stand the discomfort long enough to find a real solution.
Psychologizing	"Do you know why you said that?" "You're just being oversensitive."	To help prevent future problems by analyzing the child's behavior and explaining his motives.	"I know more about you than you know about yourself. Therefore, I'm superior to you.
Being Judgmental	"Why were you doing that in the first place?" "That wasn't a very smart thing to do."	To help the child realize what she did wrong.	"You have poor judgment. You don't make good decisions.
Sarcasm	"Well, I guess that's just about the end of the world."	To show the child how wrong her attitudes or behavior are by making her feel ridiculous.	"You are ridiculous."
Moralizing	"The right thing to do would be..." "You really should..."	To show the child the proper way to deal with the problem.	"I'll choose your values for you."
Being a Know-It-All	"Everybody knows that when something like this happens, you..."	To show the child that he has a resource for handling any problem—you.	"Since I know it all, you must know nothing."

49

Active Communication

Instead of blocking communication, you can use "active communication," a set of skills that will help you win cooperation and support your child in solving problems. Active communication is recommended when your child owns a problem you'd like to help her solve, or when you both share responsibility for a problem. There are five steps:

Step 1	**Listen actively.**
Step 2	**Listen for feelings.**
Step 3	**Connect feelings to content.**
Step 4	**Look for alternatives and evaluate consequences.**
Step 5	**Follow up later.**

1. Listen actively.

What do I mean by "active" listening? If you listen fully, you don't just receive information; you are an active participant in the communication process. You listen with your eyes as well as your ears, with your intuition as well as your thinking. With active listening, you're trying to encourage your child to express what he is thinking and feeling. Here's how:

Give full attention. Your child may feel encouraged by the attention alone. It says, "I care about you. You matter. I'm here to help."

Keep your own talk to a minimum. When your mouth is open, your ears don't work as well. So listen, and don't talk a lot.

Acknowledge what you are hearing. Let your child know that you are understanding, that you are taking her words to heart. You can say something as simple as "I see" now and then or even "Uh-huh." Ask questions to clarify what your child is saying or to summarize long stories.

2. Listen for feelings.

Listen to what your child is feeling about her perception of the facts.

Most parents make the mistake of only listening to the content of the child's story. While getting the facts straight is important, it is even more important to listen to what your child is feeling about her perception of the facts. This will help your child acknowledge and accept his feelings rather than keep them bottled up. Some children ignore their painful feelings for so long that they eventually act them out aggressively or suffer from stress-related sickness such as stomachaches or headaches. Part of developing his emotional intelligence is to teach him to say how he feels and then to reflect on his feelings before he decides what action to take.

Until a child has been taught to describe his feelings with words, you will have to listen closely to his tone of voice and watch his face to discover what he is feeling. Then name his feeling in your own mind.

Examples:

> *"This is a really scary situation for Lizzie."*
> *"Raymond sounds really angry."*
> *"She's worried about what the other kids think about her weight."*

Allow yourself to feel some of what your child is feeling.

This type of listening is sometimes called "listening with empathy." **Empathy** means sharing another person's feelings. Allow yourself to feel some of what your child is feeling. This will help you connect with her in a way that shows how much you care, an essential quality in helping someone with an emotionally charged problem. The result of such empathetic listening is usually an increased willingness on the part of the child to continue sharing.

3. Connect feelings to content.

When you have actively listened to what your child has to say and have an idea of what he is feeling, the next step is to reflect those feelings back to him. You can become what psychologist Haim Ginott calls an "emotional mirror." They just reflect what is there. Reflect the feelings and then connect them to what happened—the "content." By responding this way, you communicate the most powerful message of all: You care. Because the content is sometimes obvious, you can often simply respond to the feeling and accomplish the same empathy without sounding like you are repeating what he has just told you.

Examples:

> *"This storm can be pretty scary, can't it Lizzie?"* OR
> *"You seem a little scared, Lizzie."*
> *"You sound really angry that you weren't invited, Raymond."* OR
> *"I can hear how angry you are."*

> *"Samantha, you seem worried about what the other kids think about your weight."* or
>
> *"You seem worried, Samantha."*

By reflecting feelings in tentative terms ("It sounds as though…" or "I guess…") you don't come across like you're trying to be a mind-reader or a know-it-all. If you miss your guess about what your child is feeling, she can correct you. That way you're sure you understand what she is saying and feeling.

Example:

> ***Samantha:*** *No…it's not that. I just don't think they should call me names. It's mean.*
>
> ***Mother:*** *I see. You're more angry than worried.*

By adjusting to the child's correction, the communication continues to flow.

When you reflect the feeling accurately, an exciting thing will happen. Your child will nod her head in recognition, maybe say "yes," and then continue to share. She will feel understood and cared for—and she may understand herself a little better.

Connecting Feelings to Content

What the Child Says	Feeling Word	What the Parent Says
"Mom, I'm not going to do Jon's dishes again!"	Angry	"You seem angry that I want you to clean all the dishes."
"I missed the foul shot, and we lost the game."	Disappointment	"Sounds like you're really disappointed about that."
"This shirt is so diumb."	Embarrassed	"I guess you're embarrassed about what the other kids will think."
"She invited Caitlyn to her slumber party, but not me!"	Hurt	"Oh, I bet that really hurts your feelings."

4. Look for alternatives and evaluate consequences.

After each alternative that your child comes up with you can help predict the consequences.

Helping children become effective problem solvers is one of the skills that will enable them to survive and thrive in our fast-changing 21st century. Because most children will immediately rush to try whatever solution pops into their minds, our job is to slow them down by helping them look at various options and then predicting the likely consequences of each. You can begin by asking such simple questions as:

> *"What can you do about that?"*
> *"What else could you try?"*

After each alternative that your child comes up with you can help predict the consequences by asking:

> *"What do you think would happen if you did that?"*

It is better for your child to think of alternatives on her own without your prompting. This helps her develop her own problem solving skills and the persistence to keep thinking when solutions do not come easily. It also keeps her from being able to blame you if a solution does not work out well, which strengthens her sense of responsibility. However, when a child cannot think of a solution herself, you can sometimes gently suggest some. Be very careful in these cases not to take over or otherwise seem to be insisting that she do it your way. Remember, she owns the problem and your role is that of a helpful consultant who makes suggestions, but does not dictate solutions. You might simply ask, "Would you like to know what others in such a situation have done?"

Remember, if the child owns the problem, then your role is that of a helpful consultant.

This is also a good time to use the **"palms up" technique.** By actually turning your palms up and saying, "I don't know what you will decide to do, but what if…," you can leave the final decision in your child's hands. This method lowers resistance and actually allows you to be more of an influence in the long run than if you pointed a finger and said, "Here's what you should do…"

Another non-threatening way of introducing an alternative is through your own self-disclosure. If you faced a similar situation in your own childhood, you can share the story and include any successful solutions that you found.

Example:

> *"That reminds me of a time when I wasn't invited to a party that I really wanted to go to. I sat around feeling hurt for awhile, but then I decided that I wasn't going to let the girl that was giving it ruin my whole day. So I called a friend of mine from another school and we spent the day together having a great time."*

Be careful not to turn this into a lecture of the "when-I-was-child-I walked-five-miles-through-the-snow" type. Remember, too, that your child is free to use or not use your ideas as she thinks best. Unless her solution is unsafe or violates your family values, you have to remain accepting even if she chooses an alternative that you think will fail. After all, she owns the problem. Plus, there is a lot to be learned from failed ideas.

Finally, ask your child what he intends to do, and when. Do this gently, and if he is not ready to commit to a course of action, keep in mind that even Einstein often needed time for ideas to incubate before deciding what to do next.

5. Follow-up later.

A tremendous amount is gained by talking about a solution to a problem after it has been tried. Make sure you remember to ask your child how he handled the problem and what kind of results followed. This follow-up not only helps your child learn from the experience, but also validates that your interest was genuine. If the results were good, then a little encouragement is all that is required. However, if the problem still exists, or new ones were created, then you can begin the active communication process all over again to find another solution.

Examples:

> *"How did it go with…?"*
>
> *"Remember that talk we had about _____ the other day? I was wondering how it turned out."*

Putting Active Communication to Work

Now that you are aware of the five steps of the active communication process, look for opportunities to use them to help your child solve her own problems. You'll find that the more supportive you are, the more cooperative your child is likely to be.

If you are having a lot of friction with your child, however, he may not yet be willing to sit down for a long discussion. You can still listen for his feelings and express your empathy.

Examples:

"Boy, you sure look down."

"I guess you're really ticked off."

"That must have hurt."

You can even use this skill when disciplining your child or telling him he can't do something. It may help reduce his anger. Just having his feelings recognized and accepted can sometimes help.

Examples:

"I know you're angry that I won't let you stay up later."

"I'm sorry my decision feels so bad to you."

"If looks could kill, I'd be in real trouble right now."

"I can live with you not liking me very much right now, but I don't think I could live with myself if something terrible happened to you."

Feeling Words

Although the English language has hundreds of words that describe specific feelings, most people do not use many in their daily vocabulary. As you practice looking for the right "feeling words," you will find your feeling word vocabulary increases and the job gets easier. To help with this process, we have included a list of feeling words for you to keep in mind.

WORDS THAT DESCRIBE PLEASANT FEELINGS		WORDS THAT DESCRIBE UNPLEASANT FEELING	
Accepted	Hopeful	Afraid	Jealous
Adequate	Honored	Angry	Let down
Adventurous	Important	Anxious	Lonely
Bold	Joyful	Ashamed	Miserable
Brilliant	Lovely	Bashful	Nervous
Calm	Loving	Bored	Overwhelmed
Caring	Overjoyed	Cautious	Pained
Cheerful	Peaceful	Cheated	Possessive
Comfortable	Peppy	Concerned	Provoked
Confident	Playful	Defeated	Pushed
Content	Pleased	Defiant	Rejected
Daring	Proud	Disappointed	Remorseful
Eager	Refreshed	Discouraged	Resentful
Elated	Relieved	Down	Shy
Encouraged	Satisfied	Embarrassed	Stupid
Energetic	Secure	Envious	Suspicious
Fascinated	Successful	Frustrated	Trapped
Free	Surprised	Guilty	Uncomfortable
Full	Sympathetic	Hateful	Uneasy
Glad	Tranquil	Hesitant	Unhappy
Great	Understood	Hopeless	Unloved
Gutsy	Warm	Hurt	Unsure
Happy	Wonderful	Impatient	Weary
High	Zany	Irritated	Worried

Family Enrichment Activity:
Bedtime Routines and I Love You's

Children, particularly young children, want and need a lot of structure in their days. Knowing that certain things happen at certain times and in certain ways offers a sense of security and order to their worlds. As they get older, they can develop their own structures, and can depend on us less.

As with most things, moderation is still a key. A rigid structure that can never vary is just as bad as a structure that is so flexible children never know what they can count on.

One of the best structures you can develop for your children is a bedtime routine. Many parents experience conflict at bedtime, and it doesn't have to be that way. Like many of the problems that have been discussed in this program, we can use the active style of parenting to turn bedtime into a positive time of day. Remember to:

> 1. **Make it a win/win for both of you.** You can help make the bedtime routine more acceptable to your children if you look for ways to involve them in the process and to make it fun.
>
> 2. **Encourage…encourage…encourage.**

One of the best structures you can develop for your children is a bedtime routine.

Bedtime can be one of the happiest times of the day for both you and your children—if you make it fun and involving. Here is a good routine that has been successful in many families with young children:

Begin with bath time. Bath time can easily be experienced as a continuation of play time for the kids when you add a little music, some bathtub toys, and make it fun for yourself, too. For example:

> *"Here's the world famous diver getting ready to do a triple somersault into a tub of wet children."*

Teeth brushing. Bath time, of course, is followed by teeth brushing, which may never qualify as fun, but getting your children involved and using some encouragement can at least keep them on the right track. For example:

> *"You're doing such a good job. I really like the way you are getting to those teeth hiding way in the back."*

Bedtime story. One of the favorite bedtime routines is a bedtime story. Whether you use a book or make up your own story, this offers a pleasant transition from the active play of the day to the quiet of bedtime. One way to encourage a child who is reluctant to read is to begin a longer book, reading one chapter a night. This gives the child something to look forward to each day. With older children you might substitute some quiet talk about the events of the day instead of a story. Whatever you do during this "talk and hug time," it's an opportunity for winding down and relaxing.

Special rituals. Then it's time for lights out and your own special rituals. This might include a prayer if you like, and then other regular words or actions—a back rub, a special poem, or something you make up. For example:

> *"If all the little girls in the whole wide world were put end to end and I could choose anyone to be my daughter, I'd choose you."*

Expressing love. Building a positive relationship with children is an ongoing process, and it sometimes takes steady effort. As we have seen, it involves making arrangements to have fun together, using active communication, and showing mutual respect. Most of all, the positive relationship between parent and child involves expressing love for each other. All children hunger for love, even those who make a career of acting "unlovable." Children need to know that whatever else may happen, their parents love them. Methods of expressing love to children can be woven into the fabric of everyday life: a kiss, a pat on the back, a tousling of hair, an arm around the shoulder. But it is equally important to be able to say to your child that you love him. The words may come awkwardly for some parents. But the important thing is how beautiful they sound to children.

Parents can say, "I love you" when the child will be surprised at the timing, but pleased with the message. Parents can say "I love you" at a time of calmness or tenderness, such as bedtime, and the child can bask in the warmth of the words. For example:

"I love you."

Chapter 2

HOME ACTIVITIES

- **Complete the Communication Blocks chart on page 198.**
- **Practice Active Communication when your child owns a problem, and fill out the worksheet on page 202.**
- **Continue working on ways to take care of yourself, and continue filling out page 195.**
- **Have a family meeting on bedtime routines and put them into practice. Fill out the worksheet on page 204.**
- **Remember to say "I love you" every day.**

Responsibility and Discipline

There was a young man who was desperate for work. He had never had a job, and though he was 27 years old, his parents were still supporting him. They had finally had enough of his dependency, as well as their own overprotection, and had given him three months to find a job. When he saw after ten weeks that they were not bluffing about pushing him out of the nest, he began seriously beating the pavement for work.

He failed. He had never been taught to do things for himself and had not developed the skills to find a job. His father, as usual, came to his rescue. He called a friend in the construction business who arranged for the son to have a job driving a dump truck, a job for which he would be well paid. On the first day of his first job, the young man backed the dump truck over an embankment. When confronted by the foreman and asked how he could do such a reckless thing, the young man replied, "Well, nobody told me not to."

This chapter and the next will present methods of handling problems and misbehavior when they occur in a family. But this chapter is also about something much more basic to the development of a child's ability to thrive in our modern society. It is about responsibility.

What is Responsibility?

The young man in the story was obviously not behaving responsibly when he backed the dump truck over the hill. But what does the term "responsibility" really mean? Let's consider three definitions:

1. **Accepting one's obligations**

2. **Doing the right thing as the situation calls for it.**

3. **Accepting accountability for one's actions**

Accepting One's Obligations

Teaching our children that there are times when we must sacrifice our own short-term desires for long-term benefits is teaching them responsibility.

There are times in all of our lives when we would rather not do some things that we feel obligated to do. These "obligations" are sometimes specifically made between two people. For example, when you tell your child that you will pick her up after school, you are obligated to be there. Other obligations are made implicitly through the roles we accept in our daily lives. The job of parenting, for example, carries with it many obligations including providing food, clothing, discipline, and support. Teaching our children that there are times when we must sacrifice our own short-term desires for long-term benefits is teaching them responsibility. Childhood is filled with opportunities to teach this lesson.

Examples:

- *Owning a pet means accepting responsibility for caring for it.*
- *Being on a team means showing up for practice and games.*
- *Learning a musical instrument means practicing.*
- *Being in a family means doing chores.*
- *Being a student means doing homework and studying.*

Doing the Right Thing as the Situation Calls for It

Helping our children learn the difference between right and wrong and instilling the desire to do what is right even when it is difficult or painful, is one of the more challenging jobs of parenthood. We want our children to grow up to be good people who do right things, but often what is right is difficult to know. Sometimes doing the right thing even conflicts with the law, as was the case during the civil rights movement. At other times, the population as a whole is split about what is right and what is wrong, as in the case of abortion. Your own family values and faith will have to guide you in many such situations.

Doing the right thing is often a lot like spelling. For every rule there seems to be an exception.

Examples:

- *Do not hurt someone...unless it's in self-defense.*
- *Do not lie...unless it's a white lie to spare feelings.*
- *Work hard...but don't be a workaholic.*
- *Stand up for your friends...unless they are doing something wrong.*

Taking time to talk with your children about real life situations is the best way to help them grapple with the many nuances of right and wrong. Asking them, "What do you think is the right thing to do?" implies that in your family you strive to know what is right and to do it. When your child does the right thing, be sure to encourage her by acknowledging both the action and the courage it took to act.

Accepting Accountability for One's Actions

At the very core of responsibility is accepting that what happens to us results from decisions that we make.

At the very core of responsibility is accepting that what happens to us results from decisions that we make. It is much easier for children, as well as adults, to blame their problems on other people or circumstances, or to just make excuses. But doing so prevents them from learning how to make better decisions in the future. After all, if it wasn't their fault why should they bother to think about what they could do differently next time?

Learning to accept responsibility helps children become very creative at solving problems. Such children grow into adults who are constantly examining life and finding ways to make it work better. They become successful adults who, when they do make a mistake, accept the consequences, learn from it, and then move on. Those who never learn this lesson in responsibility often go through life making the same mistakes over and over.

Responsibility ➡ Growth ➡ Success Cycles

Why do we avoid responsibility if this is so? Because we are afraid of being blamed or punished for making mistakes. Who would blame or punish us? Sometimes it is critical people with whom we live or work. But even their criticism would be harmless if it were not for the fact that we blame and punish ourselves the most.

Where did we learn this self-criticism? Most of us learned it a long time ago from our parents, many of whom believed in the autocratic or permissive methods of parenting and the blame and criticism that went with these styles.

How do we avoid responsibility? We blame others for our mistakes and failures, or we blame circumstances, because it is too painful to accept responsibility and suffer the self-criticism we often heap on ourselves..

We say, "You made me late," or "You made me angry." Or we justify our failings: "Being late isn't such a big deal;" "I have a bad temper;" "I'm a Leo;" "I'm an alcoholic;" "I'm just no good;" "Nobody told me not to."

How can we help prepare children for responsible adulthood? The first step is for us to resist the temptation to blame and punish them for their mistakes and misbehavior. These techniques actually influence them to avoid responsibility—to blame and justify. This chapter is about other methods of disciplining children, methods that teach responsibility while they help you handle everyday problems. But first, let's look at the circumstances in which choices are made.

Freedom and the Limits to Freedom

Responsibility requires that a person be held accountable for his choices, but a choice can be made only when there is freedom to choose. For if the person is not free to choose, we have to assume that someone else has already made the choice for the person. An essential condition for responsibility, therefore, is the freedom to choose.

Without structure and limits, children do not learn responsibility.

Dictator parents give their children almost no freedom to make choices. They believe that since children lack experience, parents must make choices for them. They may want to help their children avoid the pain and pitfalls of poor choices. However, these parents stifle their child's ability to handle responsibility. The child eventually rebels against these strict limits, and yet remains inexperienced at making choices on his own. The results are the very pain and pitfalls the parent sought to avoid.

Doormat parents follow a model of parenting that resembles lawlessness. Such parents allow their children too much freedom to choose. Yet without structure and limits, children do not learn responsibility any better in these circumstances than in an autocratic home.

> *A young man executed in the electric chair for the murder of a woman and her three small children reported that he would probably do it again if he had the chance, because he came from a home where no one ever told him not to do certain things. He had grown up without limits—free to do whatever he pleased. And was he happy about this? Hardly. He chose the electric chair instead of imprisonment because he described his life as a "living hell."*

So children clamor for freedom to make their own choices while parents call for limits to that freedom, and the dialogue becomes a universal chant, repeated the world over:

"Freedom!" "Limits." "FREEDOM!" "LIMITS!"

Fortunately, there is a third alternative—"active" parenting. Active parents are acutely aware of their children's need for freedom, but freedom within well-defined limits. They work hard to set limits in line with each child's age and level of responsibility. They are aware that over-restrictive limits lead to sneaking around and other forms of rebellion, and too-loose limits lead to selfish and destructive behavior.

Freedom Within Limits

Active parents are acutely aware of their children's need for freedom, but freedom within well-defined limits.

This concept of "freedom within expanding limits" suggests that a three-year-old will make fewer of her own decisions than a ten-year-old, who again will make fewer decisions than a 17-year-old. In fact, the ideal situation for a teen spending her last year at home is for her to make almost all of her own decisions. The parent has become almost like a roommate and consultant. This makes sense when we consider that our goal is to prepare children for independent living, because we won't always be around to provide limits.

Like most things, teaching responsibility is a gradual process. It involves giving children choices and then allowing them to experience the consequences of those choices. In fact, since responsibility is a matter of accepting the consequences of our choices, then a reasonable formula for teaching responsibility to children is:

Responsibility = Choice + Consequence

What are our best opportunities for using this formula? First, we can let the child make more daily decisions. We can allow increasing freedom to make such choices as to eat and what to wear, keeping in mind the child's age and stage of development. (Refer to "The Method of Choice" section in Chapter One on page 25.) Second, when we have a problem with the child's behavior, we can look for opportunities to give her choices and allow her to experience the consequences of her actions. This combination of choice and consequence, as we will see later in this chapter, is a very effective discipline method.

Reward and Punishment Often Backfire

Discipline is important for teaching most children how to live within the limits of the situation and the values of the family. However, discipline does not necessarily mean reward and punishment. In fact, the word itself comes from the Latin word, disciplina, which means "to teach." How we choose to

teach our children right from wrong, the importance of fulfilling their obligations, and accepting responsibility for their actions can be for better or for worse.

We mentioned earlier that reward and punishment are how the dictator parent enforces his orders. Children are kept in line with the threat of punishment if they misbehave and the promise of reward if they do what the parent wants them to do. This system of reward and punishment may have been effective in older days when the world was ruled by kings, queens, and emperors and everyone "knew his place," but in a society of equals, it doesn't work very well.

REWARD: **something extra that is thrown in to bribe the child to change behavior.**

For one thing, a reward for good behavior comes to be expected almost as a right. A child does not learn to behave cooperatively just because the situation calls for it, or because the family functions better when everyone follows the rules or pitches in. Instead, he develops a "what's in it for me" attitude that leads him to expect more and more rewards for positive behavior. The parent must then increase the value of the reward to keep it effective until she reaches a point of frustration. This frustration often leads to the use of punishment.

INCENTIVE: built into the sequence of events on a regular basis and is logically connected.

In a society of equals, when you hurt someone, you give that person an unspoken right to hurt you back.

On the other hand, incentives, when used correctly as part of a logical consequence, can be very effective because, unlike rewards, they are logically connected to the situation. We'll learn more about using incentives as part of When/Then choices later in this chapter.

Punishment continues to be a popular method for many parents because it does appear to work in the short run. Under the threat of punishment children will often improve negative behavior. However, punishment is not effective in the long run because it often creates resentment on the part of the child. In a society of equals, when you hurt someone, you give that person an unspoken right to hurt you back. Children will usually find ways of getting even through future misbehavior or worse.

In fact, reward and punishment are out of place among equals. It is only a superior who can give rewards and mete out punishments, and it is only inferiors who can receive them. All in all, rewards and punishments as methods of child-rearing are holdovers from an earlier time when the world was a different place. There are much more effective methods of discipline, and we will become acquainted with them in this program.

The Think-Feel-Do Cycle

Effective discipline requires some understanding of what motivates children—why they do what they do. Let's consider four separate aspects and see how they are related: events (something that happens in the child's life); his thinking (including his beliefs, attitudes and values); his feelings; and his behavior. I call it the "think-feel-do cycle," because this is how the cycle works:

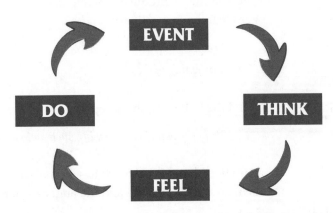

Change the thinking and you change the feelings, too.

When something happens to a child (an event), he thinks about it, both consciously and unconsciously. All of his attitudes and values about such situations and about himself come into play like data in a powerful computer. This thinking then produces a feeling. Many people mistakenly believe that feelings just happen, but they are really products of our thoughts and values. Change the thinking and you change the feelings, too. Then together, the thinking and feeling produce an action—what the child does to influence the event. As the event changes or remains the same, the child will have new thoughts, feelings, and behavior as the system goes around and around.

Example:

> *Ten-year-old Steven's mother notices that he has left the milk out on the counter and says in an angry voice, "Steven, how many times do I have to tell you to put the milk back in the refrigerator?!"*

This **event** in Steven's life triggers a lot of conscious and unconscious thoughts, including:

Here she goes on my case again.

She has no right to yell at me.

She is always mad about something.

I'm tired of her putting me down all the time.

These thoughts produce a feeling of anger and resentment, which then trigger the following actions:

A scowl

A stiffening of the back

...and the following sharp reply:

"Why are you always making such a big deal out of everything?!"

The effect that this behavior has on the event (that is, mother) triggers her own think-feel-do cycle and the angry response back:

"Well, I wouldn't have to make a big deal out of it if you'd show a little responsibility!"

This autocratic style and her punishing remark triggers Steven's rebellious attitude and thinking that "she can't treat me this way" as he storms out of the room in anger—and the cycle continues.

Of course parents aren't the only events in their children's lives. Every day is filled with many pleasant and challenging events to which kids must respond with thoughts, feelings and behavior. Some of the most dangerous of these events involve conflicts that could lead to violence and unsafe risks that could, in turn, lead to serious accidents. Later, as preteens and teens, events will take the form of offers to use tobacco, alcohol, and other drugs and to engage in risky sexual behavior, or sexual activity that violates your family values. One of our jobs as parents is to filter out as many of these unsafe events as possible. This includes such actions as:

Knowing where they are and who is supervising them

Knowing who their friends are and encouraging positive friendships

Monitoring their use of media, including the internet, TV, music, and movies

Keeping them away from unsafe people and places

(We will learn more about parents as filters in Chapter Six.)

However, since we will not always be there to act as screens, our ultimate goal is to teach children the attitudes, values, and self-esteem that will give them the courage and character to choose positive behavior later when they are faced with challenging events. Positive behavior leads to positive results, which increases self-esteem and courage leading to more positive behavior. This is called a success cycle. We will talk more about how to instill self-esteem and courage in Chapter Five, but for now let's concentrate on the overall cycle.

Success Cycle

Parents filtering out many negative events

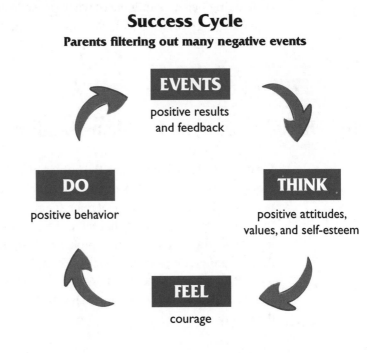

EVENTS
positive results
and feedback

THINK
positive attitudes,
values, and self-esteem

FEEL
courage

DO
positive behavior

Of course, the opposite can also occur. Negative attitudes, values, and low self-esteem can produce discouragement and negative behavior which leads to poor results and punishment. This lowers self-esteem further, producing more discouragement and negative behavior—causing a "failure cycle." The keys to teaching our children the thinking that produces a success cycle (and breaks a failure cycle) include the following:

- Treating our children respectfully and encouraging their participation as thinking human beings *(Chapter One)*

- Using active communication to talk about problems and potential problems while instilling our family values *(Chapter Two)*

- Using effective discipline to set limits and teach responsibility *(Chapters Three and Four)*

- Building self-esteem, courage and character *(Chapter Five)*

- Filtering negative influences when possible and talking about how to handle high risk events such as drugs, sexuality, and violence *(Chapter Six)*

Effective Discipline and the Problem-Handling Model

We discussed in Chapter Two the importance of using problems as teaching tools for instilling qualities of character such as cooperation, courage, and responsibility in children. Let's refer again to the Problem-Handling Model that was presented in that chapter and notice the highlighted areas. These include methods of preventing problems, and then how to handle problems that the parent owns using effective discipline. The remainder of this chapter will focus on how to use these powerful skills to teach your child responsibility and how to live within the limits that you determine as the leader in the family.

THE PROBLEM-HANDLING MODEL

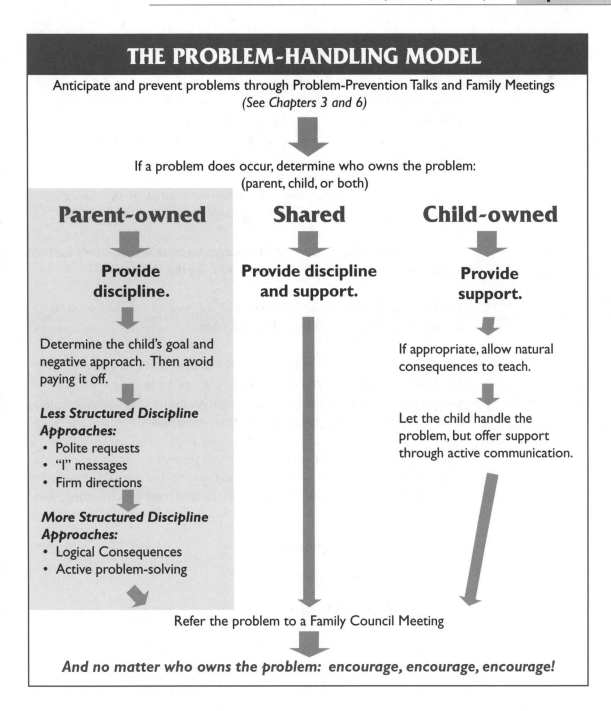

Anticipate and prevent problems through Problem-Prevention Talks and Family Meetings
(See Chapters 3 and 6)

If a problem does occur, determine who owns the problem:
(parent, child, or both)

Parent-owned

**Provide
discipline.**

Determine the child's goal and
negative approach. Then avoid
paying it off.

***Less Structured Discipline
Approaches:***
• Polite requests
• "I" messages
• Firm directions

***More Structured Discipline
Approaches:***
• Logical Consequences
• Active problem-solving

Shared

**Provide discipline
and support.**

Child-owned

**Provide
support.**

If appropriate, allow natural
consequences to teach.

Let the child handle the
problem, but offer support
through active communication.

Refer the problem to a Family Council Meeting

And no matter who owns the problem: encourage, encourage, encourage!

Effective Discipline

Of course, we won't be able to prevent all problems. At times children will become discouraged and turn to negative behavior to achieve their goals. When misbehavior occurs, discipline is often required to motivate the child to change behavior. When using any of the discipline skills that will follow, keep in mind these tips:

1. Our goal is to teach our children, not to hurt them. In fact, we can teach far better without hurting their feelings or their bottoms.

2. Whenever we discipline a child for negative behavior, we want to find opportunities to encourage any improvement the child makes.

3. When using discipline to influence our children, we always want to use the least assertive method that will work.

4. Let discipline be motivated by caring. When a child knows that you are disciplining her because you care about her, it's easier to accept. When we discipline out of frustration, anger, and our own desires, it's difficult for the child to accept or "learn" the lesson we're trying to teach.

The first three discipline methods that we will present are basic communication methods that increase in assertiveness from mild to firm. Begin with the first, and if it does not work move on to the second, and then the third. They are:

- **Polite Requests**
- **"I" Messages**
- **Firm reminders**

Polite Requests

Not every problem or conflict requires a full-fledged discussion or firm discipline. As we said before, sometimes the reason a child misbehaves is simply because they do not know what you expect of them. Often, a polite request is enough to influence a child to change behavior (especially if the relationship is already a positive one).

The first step is to politely make our desires known through a request. For example, you have decided that you no longer want to pamper your child by picking up the dirty dishes he leaves in the den. Your polite request might be:

> *"Honey, from now on will you do me a favor and bring your dishes to the sink when you're through with your snack?"*

If your child agrees, be sure to add:

> *"Thanks, that will be a big help."*

The first step is to politely make our desires known through a request.

This may seem too obvious to mention, but we parents do talk to children in ways that would be clearly disrespectful if used with other adults. The parent in the above example could easily wait until she is fed up with being a servant, hold it inside for another week to let it really boil, then burst out with "I'm sick and tired of having to pick up your mess! What do you think I am, your personal servant? If you weren't so lazy and inconsiderate ..." This kind of outburst is not likely to produce responsibility, cooperation—or dishes in the sink.

If a child does comply with our polite request, but slips up, we can offer a friendly reminder:

> *"Honey, I notice you forgot to put your dishes in the sink. Please come get them."*

When a child repeatedly forgets to keep an agreement, then a stronger communication is called for.

"I" Messages

 "I" messages, a term coined by psychologist Thomas Gordon in his pioneering Parent Effectiveness Training (P.E.T.) program, are firm and friendly communications that can produce surprisingly effective results. They are called "I" messages because they shift the emphasis from the child (a traditional "you" message) to how the parent ("I") feels about the child's behavior. "I" Messages:

- **Allow the parent to say how he or she feels about the child's behavior without blaming or labeling the child.**

- **Create a situation in which the child is more likely to hear what the parent is saying because it is expressed in a nonthreatening way.**

- **Convey clearly to the child one consequence (the parent's feeling) of the child's behavior.**

- **Put the emphasis on the child's behavior and not on the child's personality.**

- **Give the child clear information about what change in behavior the parent wants.**

When To Use an "I" Message:

When a polite request has failed to change behavior, an "I" message is a more assertive next step.

"I" messages are only effective when the parent owns the problem. When a polite request has failed to change behavior, an "I" message is a more assertive next step.

Since "I" messages work best in a firm and calm tone of voice, avoid using them when you are too angry. Allow for a cooling-off period, then approach your child when you have regained control. An angry "I" message can easily trigger rebellion in a power-seeking child.

How To Send an "I" Message:

There are four parts to an "I" message.

1. Name the behavior or situation you want changed. In order to avoid attacking a child's self esteem it is important to "separate the deed from the doer" It isn't that the child is bad, only that we have a problem with something the child is doing. By beginning with a statement aimed at the behavior, we avoid attacking the child's personality and self-esteem. We begin with "I have a problem with ..." For example:

> *"I have a problem with your leaving dirty dishes on the coffee table."*

2. Say how you feel about the situation. This lets the child know that the problem is serious to you (without raising your voice). Although parents often use the word "angry" to describe their feelings, this is often a mask for two other emotions: "fear" and "hurt." Children can usually hear us better when we are expressing these emotions because they are less threatening. "I  feel concerned" or "I feel hurt" may be closer to the truth, as well as more effective. This part of the "I" message begins with "I feel..." For example:

> *"I feel taken advantage of... "*

3. State your reason. Nobody likes to be treated as if he were expected to be blindly obedient. If we are going to change what is comfortable to us to please an authority, we at least want that authority to have a good reason. Children are no exception. A simple explanation about how the child's behavior is interfering with your needs or the needs of the situation can go a long way. For example:

> *"... because I have to spend time and energy cleaning up behind you."*

Remember, you get more of what you ask for than what you don't ask for.

4. Say what you want done. You have already made a polite request or two, so now you are getting more assertive. This means letting your child know exactly what you would like done. Remember, you get more of what you ask for than what you don't ask for. This step can begin with "I want" or "I would like." For example:

> *"I would like you to bring your dirty dishes to the kitchen and put them in the dishwasher when you leave the den."*

Putting this "I" message all together, we have:

> *"I have a problem with your leaving dirty dishes on the coffee table. I feel taken advantage of because I have to spend time and energy cleaning up behind you. I would like you to bring your dirty dishes to the kitchen and put them in the dishwasher when you leave the den."*

Making "I" Messages Stronger: Two Variations

1. Getting agreement. "Will you please ..." We can make an "I" message even stronger by getting an agreement from the child about the behavior we want changed. This can be done by simply adding the question, "Will you do that?" and then not moving until you get a "yes." Saying "yes" verbally commits the child to action and helps motivate her to follow through later. This can also be done by changing the last step of the "I" message from "I would like ..." to "Will you please ..." For example:

> *"I have a problem with your leaving dirty dishes on the coffee table. I feel taken advantage of because I have to spend time and energy cleaning up behind you. Will you please bring your dirty dishes to the kitchen and put them in the dishwasher when you are finished? Will you do that?"*

2. Establishing a time frame. "When?" Every parent knows the frustrations of getting an agreement from a child about doing something, finding it still not done hours later, and confronting the child only to hear the refrain, "I'll do it." The implication, of course, is "I'll do it when I get around to it," and that may not occur in this decade.

The solution is to get a clear agreement as to when the behavior will be completed. In the above example, the "when" is built into the phrase "when you are finished." Other times, it can be added right after the child agrees to the request by simply asking, "When?"

Firm Directions

If your child does not respond to a polite request or an "I" Message, your next step is to give a short, but firm, reminder. By suspending the rules of grammar and syntax, you give the message additional "oomph."

Example:

> *"Dishes. Sink. Now."*

The fewer words you use the better. This means avoiding the temptation to give a mini lecture on responsibility while your child sits there ignoring you. Just make solid eye-contact and firmly remind your child about what you want done.

Make solid eye-contact and firmly remind your child about what you want done.

Your child may very well spring into action, amazing you and surprising himself in the process. If so, build on this success, as always by encouraging him with a thank-you. However, some kids seem to need a lot of reminders, in which case it may be time to move on to the more advanced discipline methods: the rack and the screw. (Just kidding! These methods have been replaced in this edition with logical consequences and active problem solving.)

Logical Consequences

In order to influence a child to change from a negative behavior to a positive one, the child first needs clear information from the parent about what change is expected. The basic discipline methods just covered provide the clear, firm communication to do this. However, children sometimes need to experience a more concrete consequence of their actions in order to learn the lesson of responsibility. Remember:

Responsibility = Choice + Consequence

Consequences are powerful teachers about the effectiveness of our choices and behavior.

We have already seen how reward and punishment as consequences can often backfire. The use of logical consequences offers an advanced form of discipline that is more consistent with life in a modern democratic society. A logical consequence can be defined like this:

> *Discipline that is logically connected to a misbehavior and applied by an authority to influence a child to behave within the limits of the situation.*

Consequences are powerful teachers about the effectiveness of our choices and behavior. Better than a punishment or lecture, consequences offer parents their prime discipline tools. There are two types of consequences: natural consequences and logical consequences. We'll cover natural consequences in Chapter Five. For now we'll concentrate on logical consequences.

Examples:

> *When Sean continues to forget to bring his dirty dishes into the kitchen after snacking in the den, he loses the privilege of taking food out of the kitchen.*
>
> *When Carly refuses to put away her toys, her mother puts them in the closet, out of reach, for the next day.*
>
> *When Dennis The Menace® uses crayon on the wall, he must use his time and energy to wash it off.*

Born Again

Dennis the Menace ® used by permission of Hank Ketchum and © by North American Syndicate.

Logical Consequences Vs. Punishment

Logical consequences are not the same thing as punishment, even though the child will usually experience both as unpleasant. Some of the differences include:

LOGICAL CONSEQUENCES	PUNISHMENT
are logically connected to the misbehavior	is an arbitrary retaliation for misbehavior
are intended to teach responsible behavior	is intended to teach blindly obedient behavior
are administered in a firm and calm manner	is often delivered in an atmostphere of anger and resentment
are respectful	is disrespectful
allow the child to participate	is dictated by the authority

Types of Logical Consequences

Learning how to handle responsibility is learning how to make good decisions. Logical consequences should therefore always be presented in the form of a choice. The consequences of children's choices teach them how to make better choices in the future. Parents can help children in this learning process by showing them that misbehavior is one of their choices, but that it brings with it logical consequences. It should also be emphasized to the child that a positive choice will bring about positive consequences.

There are two types of choices you will find extremely useful:

- **Either-or choices: "Either you may ... or you may ... You decide."**

- **When-then choices: "When you have ... then you may ..."**

Either/Or Choices

Either/or choices are particularly effective when you want your child to stop a misbehavior:

> (Katherine leaves her belongings scattered around the kitchen in the afternoon.) *"Katherine, either put your things away when you come home from school, or I'll put them in a box in the basement. You decide."*

Notice that the logical consequence of leaving her belongings lying around is the inconvenience of having to dig them out of a junk box in the basement.

> (Calvin continues to forget to put his dirty clothes in the hamper.) *"Calvin, either put your dirty clothes in the hamper, or wash them yourself. You decide."*

The logical consequence of not putting his dirty clothes in the hamper is that he must do his own wash ... or wear dirty clothes.

When/Then Choices

When/then choices are effective when you want to motivate your child to start a behavior:

> (Maria has trouble getting her homework done but likes to spend time chatting online with her friends.) *"Maria, when you have finished your homework, then you may go online."*

Notice that the logical consequence of not doing her homework is losing the privilege of using the computer. However, by phrasing the consequence positively, as a when/then choice, the options are more attractive to the child and she is more likely to be motivated to finish the homework.

(Tom is about to go play in the backyard, ignoring his regular Saturday chore of cleaning his room.) *"Tom, when you have cleaned your room, then you may go play outside."*

It is easy to accidentally turn a logical consequence into a punishment. The following examples are poorly expressed because they are couched in negative terms: "Don't do that or else..." They can easily be seen as punishment—especially when accompanied by a harsh tone of voice and aggressive body language.

It is easy to accidentally turn a logical consequence into a punishment.

Poor:

> *"Katherine, put your things away or I'm going to throw them in a box in the basement!"*
>
> *"Calvin, if you don't start putting your dirty clothes in the hamper, you're going to have to wash them yourself."*
>
> *"Tom, you may not go play outside until you have cleaned your room."*

Guidelines for Using Logical Consequences

The following guidelines will help ensure that you are really using logical consequences and not punishment. They may seem like a lot to remember, but as you practice using them they will become second nature.

1. Ask the child to help set the consequences. Since life in our democratic society requires the participation of all those concerned with a problem, we stand a much better chance that a child will cooperate with our authority if we include her in the decision-making process. You may be surprised how often the child will come up with choices and solutions that we wouldn't have thought of alone. For example:

> *"Katherine, I still have a problem with you leaving your belongings all over the kitchen. What do you think we can do to solve it?"*

One key to the success of logical consequences is that the consequence is logically connected to the misbehavior.

Even if the child has no helpful suggestions or is uncooperative about finding a solution, the important thing is that you asked. Since you have invited the child's participation, she will be less likely to think of you as a dictator and to rebel against your authority. Of course, you will want to come to the discussion prepared with your own logical consequences in case your child has no ideas.

2. Give the child a choice. If the child has a choice in the matter, she is much more likely to choose the positive behavior. Use either/or and when/then choices. Remember, either/or choices work well when you want to stop a misbehavior, and when/then choices are useful when you want to encourage a positive behavior.

3. Make sure the consequences are really logical. One key to the success of logical consequences is that the consequence is logically connected to the misbehavior. Children are better able to see the justice of such consequences and will usually accept them without resentment. However, if the consequence you select is not really related to the child's behavior, it will come across as a punishment.

Not Logical:

"Either come in to dinner when I call or no TV for a week."
"Either play quietly while I work or I'm not taking you to the movie we planned."
"Either stop fighting or you'll both get a spanking."

Logical:

"Either come in to dinner when I call or it will get cold—and you may miss it altogether."
"When it gets quiet enough for me to finish my work, then I'll continue so that we'll be able to make the movie."
"Either stop fighting or you'll have to play in separate rooms."

4. Only give choices you can live with. There are many potential logical consequences for any given problem. For that reason, brainstorming with other parents, a spouse, or even the child can help. However, when you own the problem, it is up to you to decide which choices to give your child. Only give choices you as a parent can accept.

For example, if your child continues to forget to put his dishes in the dishwasher, a choice might be:

> *"Either put your dishes in the dishwasher, or I'll leave them in the sink and there will be no clean dishes."*

However, if you know a sink full of dirty dishes will drive you crazy, then don't give him this choice. Why? Because you will likely sabotage the consequences by getting angry at him as the dishes pile up. In addition, your own values and desires are important. It is much better to keep thinking until you can come up with a consequence that won't punish you. For example:

> *"Either put your dirty dishes in the dishwasher or hire me as your waitress to do it for you."*

> *"Either put your dirty dishes in the dishwasher, or I will serve the next meal without dishes."*

By the way, parents who have used the above consequence say it takes only one meal of spaghetti eaten off a bare table by hand to teach the lesson. However, once again, if you couldn't live with the mess, then don't give this particular choice. What works for one family may not be acceptable for another.

It is essential that you remain both firm and calm.

5. Keep your tone firm and calm. When giving the choice, as well as later when you enforce the consequence, it is essential that you remain both firm and calm. An angry tone of voice (the dictator's pitfall) invites rebellion and a fight. On the other hand, a wishy-washy tone of voice (the doormat's pitfall) suggests to the child that you don't really mean what you say. This invites noncompliance. In a democratic society, a firm and calm tone used by an authority figure says, " I recognize that you have a right to be treated respectfully, but you are out-of-bounds here. My job is to help you learn to stay in bounds, and I plan to do my job."

6. Give the choice one time, then act to enforce the consequence. For a logical consequence to teach a lesson, it must be enforced. If the child continues to choose to misbehave, then immediately follow through with the consequences. One way or another, children always choose. Even if they don't respond verbally, their behavior will tell you what choice has been made. Do not give the choice a second time without putting the consequences into effect immediately. The child must see that the choice results in a consequence, and the lesson must be clear, or the value is diminished. For example:

> *"If your books were in the kitchen when I cleaned, then you will find them in the junk box in the basement."*

The child is actually testing to see if we will really do what we say we will do.

7. Expect testing. When you attempt to redirect a child's misbehavior from negative choices towards positive ones, expect her to continue to misbehave for a while. We call this testing, because the child is actually testing to see if we will really do what we say we will do. In other words, will we change our behavior? Whether we realize it or not, she was getting some payoff from our old way of respond-

ing, and she will likely try to get us to revert to what we usually do. Even a punishment, as we will see in the next chapter, can have a hidden pay off. The active parent will therefore expect that the child may continue to misbehave for awhile as a test of our commitment to change the game. If we consistently enforce the consequences, she will soon see that her testing isn't working and will change her behavior. After all, children don't continue doing what doesn't work.

8. Allow the child to try again after experiencing the consequences. Since the goal is for the child to learn from the consequences of his choice, opportunities must be provided to try again—but only after the child has experienced the logical consequence. For example, Tom has agreed that when he has cleaned his room on Saturdays, then he may go play outside. Dad sees Tom heading out the back door before the room is cleaned and reminds him of his obligation.

If the child repeats the misbehavior after experiencing the consequences, then he may be testing. One can meet this challenge by letting the consequences operate a little longer after the second try, and longer yet after the third. For example, if Tom starts heading outside again next week without doing his chores, Dad can say:

"It seems that you have decided not to play outside this morning Take care of your room and we can try again this afternoon.."

Logical Consequences Guidelines

1. Ask the child to help

2. Give the child a choice.

   • Either/Or Choice

   • When/Then Choice.

3. Make sure the consequence is logical.

4. Give choices you can live with.

5. Keep your tone firm and calm.

6. Give the choice one time, then act.

7. Expect testing.

8. Allow the child to try again later.

Family Meeting: Problem-Prevention Talk

Many conflicts and misunderstandings can be prevented if we will take the time to discuss guidelines and expectations before the situation occurs.

Children often misbehave simply because they don't know what we expect from them. In other words, they don't know where the limits are and how much freedom they are allowed. Of course, many a shrewd child will intentionally stay in the dark about the rules, operating on the belief that "it is easier to gain forgiveness than permission." In either case, many conflicts and misunderstandings can be prevented if we will take the time to discuss guidelines and expectations before the situation occurs.

As the parent you will have certain limits that are non-negotiable.

Problem prevention is not about laying down the law or telling your child about your guidelines. You will find that you can be much more effective if you will discuss potential problems together and decide on the needs of the situation. Of course, as the parent you will have certain limits that are non-negotiable, but a willingness to be flexible within those limits can go a long way to winning cooperation and avoiding problems.

Example:

You have decided to take your five-year-old grocery shopping with you. Talking with her before you leave home can improve your chances for having a problem-free outing and may save you a lot of time—and stress—in the store.

Here are some tips for such a prevention discussion:

1. Identify potential problems and risks. If you have been in similar situations before, then you probably know where the trouble spots will be. Otherwise, use your experience of similar situations and your knowledge of your child to anticipate the problems.

For example, your child often whines for a toy whenever you are in a store. He also has a tendency to wander off, forcing you to chase after him.

2. Share thoughts and feelings. Ask your child what he thinks about the situation and what problems might arise. You may be surprised that he also has concerns. Then make clear your own thoughts and feelings in a friendly manner.

For example, your child may feel that shopping is boring and he'd rather be outside playing. You might say that you understand that shopping is boring for him, but that you need to buy food for the family to eat.

Talk with your child about what is expected.

3. Generate guidelines for behavior (making the situation a win-win for both of you.) Using the information you gathered in step two, talk with your child about what is expected. When discussing guidelines, keep in mind that it is easier to comply with the rules if you enjoy the situation. We aren't suggesting the use of rewards or bribes for cooperative behavior, but rather to include some incentives.

For example, avoid:

"If you'll be good, I'll buy you a toy." This is a bribe or a reward, and will lead to having to buy the child something every time you go to the store.

Better:

"If we finish our shopping by 4:30, we'll have time to stop by the park on the way home."

Best:

> *"How would you like to help me do the shopping by handing me the groceries off the shelf? Maybe you can help me decide some things you'd like to have for dinner."*
>
> *"Great! I also need for you to stay beside me all the time so that you'll be safe and we won't interfere with other shoppers."*

For more challenging kids, however, consequences are very helpful when done right.

4. Decide on logical consequences for violating the guidelines (if necessary). Your child will be more likely to follow the guidelines if he knows what will happen if he violates a guideline. You don't need to use this step with children who are basically cooperative or who have not had problems in similar situations. In fact, such a warning may seem like an insult to a child who only needs to be included in the discussion and have his needs considered in order to cooperate. For more challenging kids, however, consequences are very helpful when done right.

For example:

> *When we get to the store you will either need to stay with me or else I'll have to put you in the cart.*

5. Follow-up later. In situations in which you are not around to ensure that the guidelines were followed, you will need to check up to see how your child behaved. If she has followed the guidelines then you can encourage her by acknowledging the good effort. If she has not, then you will need to enforce the logical consequences.

For example:

> *Karen, we agreed that you would put away your toys before dinner or else I would take them away for two days. I just want to let you know that you can have your toys back on Monday.*

Family Enrichment Activity: Positive "I" Messages.

We saw earlier in this chapter that "I" messages offer parents an effective way to confront their children about repeated misbehavior. They are clear, firm, calm communications that are often easy for children to hear without becoming defensive. These same features also make it possible to use "I" messages as encouraging statements when children are behaving well. Positive "I" messages, as we call them, can help motivate a child to continue improving her behavior.

For example, we saw how Dennis the Menace's mother used a logical consequence to teach her son not to paint on the walls. Let's say she "catches him being good" and wants to offer some encouragement. She can use a positive "I" message like this:

1. **State what you like.**
   "I really like the way you are using paper for your art project."

2. **Say how you feel.**
   "I feel good knowing that you heard what I said about the walls…"

3. **Tell them why.**
   "…because now we can have clean walls and some creative art work."

4. **Offer to do something for him.**
   "How about if we tape your picture over here like a painting in a museum?"

You may have noticed that this fourth step is slightly different than with the other "I" message. When we use an "I" message to discipline, the fourth step is to tell the child the behavior change that we want. Now that we have that change, we want to encourage his effort by making it a win/win. Just make sure that this doesn't become a reward. It will help to keep the offer logically connected to their positive behavior as Dennis's mother did in the previous example. You might even think of this as a "positive logical consequence." For example:

After using "I" messages and logical consequences to decrease the fighting between your children, you catch them cooperating. At the end of your positive "I" message, you let them know that their cooperation has let you get your work done faster so now you have time to make some popcorn, play with them, or teach them how to play a new game.

Don't worry if you don't use every step of the positive "I" message every time. The first statement alone (telling them what you like) is a good use of encouragement by itself. And feel free to use your own words so that the message feels natural to you.

Chapter 3

HOME ACTIVITIES

- Practice using polite requests, "I" messages, and firm directions, and fill out the worksheet on page 205.
- Practice using a Logical Consequence and complete the worksheet on page 207.
- Have a Problem-Prevention Talk to address a potential problem in your family. Fill in the worksheet on page 208.
- Family Enrichment Activity: Use a positive "I" message to encourage your child's improvement or other positive behavior, and complete the worksheet on page 209.
- Remember to "take care of the caregiver" and add to your chart on page 195.

There is a story about a mother who had twins. One of the children was outgoing and happy and always saw the bright side of life. The other, introverted and sad, always saw the negative. The mother did not understand her two children and so she took them to see a child psychologist. After the initial visit, the psychologist proposed an experiment to see how far the differences between the children went. He put the pessimistic, sad child in a room filled with dozens of exciting toys. The other child, optimistic and happy, was put in a room knee deep in horse manure.

After 30 minutes, the psychologist went into the first room and found the little pessimist crying amidst his toys. "But I wanted a scooter and there aren't any!" He then went into the second room where the little optimist was busily digging through the manure. He seemed excited and joyful, which baffled the psychologist. "Why are you so happy?" asked the psychologist. "Well," replied the little optimist, "with all this manure there just has to be a pony in here someplace, and I'm going to find it!"

Understanding children is often frustrating. When you were a child, did your parents ever indicate their frustration with you by saying such things as:

> *"I just don't understand you!"*
> *"Why do you do things like that?"*
> *"What were you thinking?!"*

The purpose of this chapter is to help you develop an understanding of how and why your own children behave as they do. We will then apply that understanding to the methods of active parenting that we have been learning to help you redirect them towards positive behavior when they choose to misbehave. We begin with some basic information about child development.

How Children Develop

A newborn baby is small, helpless, and absolutely dependent on someone else for her own survival. Someone else must feed, clothe, cuddle, and comfort the infant. He cannot survive alone. How does such a helpless creature develop into an independent adult with a healthy lifestyle and a personality of her own? There have been many theories about this, but these two are the most well-known:

The nature theory. Some experts believe that hereditary factors, transmitted from parents to children through genes and chromosomes, play the major role in forming the child's personality. With this view one could conclude that a child's development is decided by the biological package with which he or she is born. This theory says that physical, mental, and emotional factors existing at birth mold the personality into its unique shape. When a child misbehaves according to this theory it is due to his "nature."

The nurture theory. Other experts believe that environmental influences such as the child's home, school, neighborhood, parents, nurturing, and other experiences play the dominant role in shaping the personality. With this view, one could conclude that the child is like a lump of clay, whose development is shaped by outside influences and his unique personality is the result. When a child misbehaves according to this theory it is because of what he has learned from his environment.

The child is not a victim of heredity or circumstance but is self-determining and creative.

An active theory. But there is another school of thought that holds that while heredity and environment are important influences on personality, it is the way the child responds to or uses these influences that determines the personality. In this view, the person is not passive but active. The child is not a victim of heredity or circumstance but is self-determining and creative, building a unique personality, whether he realizes it or not, by the way he responds—by the choices he makes—to whatever influences come along. The child's destiny is not left up to fate, but is a matter of choice. We are each responsible for who we are and what we do. It is not what we have that is important, but what we do with what we have. History is filled with examples of individuals who overcame difficult handicaps to lead satisfying lives and become contributing members of their communities.

This does not mean that heredity and environment do not influence our personality and behavior. These influences are the "building blocks" that individuals use to shape their lives. Since better "building blocks" will more likely result in a more successful person, it is useful to consider these influences more closely. Some of these building blocks are heredity, family atmosphere, family constellation, and methods of parenting.

A Look at the "Building Blocks" of Personality

Heredity. The biological package the child inherits from her parents is an important resource the child uses to build a personality. This includes obvious traits such as eye color, hair type, height, body type, and other aspects of appearance. But it also includes aptitudes for various skills such as art, music, sports, math, science, language, and many others. Of course, whether these aptitudes are fully developed depends on factors in the environment and how hard the child chooses to work at developing them. The same is also true of intelligence. It is likely that nature gives us each a range of intellectual functioning, and where we wind up in that range depends on how we are stimulated by our environment and how we apply ourselves. Finally, nature seems to also give us certain temperaments. Some kids are naturally more aggressive (and challenging to parents!) than others. Some are more compliant. Some are outgoing while others tend to be introverted. As with other biological factors, temperament is modified by the child depending on how he views the environment. For example, depending on other influences and the child's own choices, a child with an aggressive temperament can grow up to be a bully and then a violent criminal—or he can learn to channel his aggressiveness positively and become a successful leader, athlete, or businessperson, to name a few possibilities.

The biological package the child inherits from her parents is an important resource the child uses to build a personality.

Family Atmosphere. For the young child, the family is the world. Almost all of the child's early influences come from the family. The kind of atmosphere that exists in the family's home is therefore very important. What does it feel like to live in the home? Is there a feeling of mutual respect and cooperation? Are family members' rights respected? Are the parents warm and caring? Is there good humor? Is there time for fun? Are girls "sugar and spice" and boys "rotten, made of cotton"? Whatever atmosphere prevails, the child will respond to it, and the responses could take many forms: optimism, pessimism, cheerfulness, shyness, curiosity, rebelliousness, and on and on. The possible responses to the day-to-day atmosphere in the family world are endless, and the child uses them as building blocks in the construction of his personality.

The kind of atmosphere that exists in the family's home is therefore very important.

Family Constellation. Another influence on your child is the number of other children in the family and the order of birth. No two children come into exactly the same family. For example, a firstborn child comes into a family consisting of two adults (sometimes only one adult). The second child enters a family made up of adults and a child. The child's position in the family influences the role she chooses to play in that family and in the world in general. There are some typical responses most first children, or most youngest children, or most middle children have to their situations. The chart on the next page shows some of these responses. They illustrate yet another way in which children—by using the building block of the family constellation—choose to form their personalities. The chart also shows some ways in which parents can avoid magnifying the negative aspects of these characteristics.

No two children come into exactly the same family.

In using the chart, keep in mind that when more than five years exist between any two children, the effect is as if there were two separate families. For example:

> *Lisa (16) treated as if an "only" child; Jason (9) treated as if a "first" child; and Susan (7) treated as if a "second" child*

Family Constellation Chart

First Child	• Often takes responsibility for other siblings • Gets along well with authority figures • Likely to become a high achiever ✓ • Needs to feel right, perfect, superior ✓	• Avoid pressure to succeed. • Encourage the fun of participating, not the goal of winning. • Teach that "mistakes are for learning." • Show "how to be gentle with yourself" when accepting failure.
Only Child	• Used to being the center of attention • Unsure of self in many ways • May feel incompetent compared to others (e.g., parents) • Likely to be responsible • Often refuses to cooperate if fails to get own way	• Provide learning opportunities with other children. • Encourage visiting friends. • Have spend-the-night company. • Use childcare and nursery schools.
Second Child	• May try to catch up with older child's competence • May try to be older child's opposite in many ways • May rebel in order to find own place	• Encourage child's uniqueness. • Avoid comparisons with oldest. • Allow second child to handle his own conflicts with the oldest.
Middle Child	• May feel crowded out, unsure of position • May be sensitive, bitter, or revengeful • May be a good diplomat or mediator	• Make time for one-on-one activities. • Include in family functions. • Ask for her opinion.
Youngest Child	• Often spoiled by parents and older siblings • Often kept a baby • Often self-indulgent • Often highly creative • Often clever	• Do not do for the youngest (especially on a regular basis) what he can do alone. • Don't rescue from conflicts (thus making a victim). • Don't refer to as "the baby." • Encourage self-reliance.

Family Constellation

As the chart shows, family constellation is another important building block. But this is important to understand: It is not so much the child's position in the family, but his view of the position that matters and makes a difference in the way he develops his personality. You and your children may or may not fit these typical characteristics, depending on decisions you have made.

The influence over which parents have the most control is their own style of parenting. Let's review the three possible styles or methods that we discussed in Chapter One:

1. Autocratic Style (The Dictator). The dictator parent is an all-powerful figure who uses reward and punishment as tools for keeping everyone in line. Children are told what, how, where, and when to do everything. There is very little room for them to question, challenge, or make their own decisions.

2. Permissive Style (The Doormat). The doormat parent allows the children to "do their own thing" too often. There are few limits placed on children and little respect for order and routine. Many permissive parents behave as doormats, allowing their children to walk all over them. In such a system, children experience insecurity because there is no feeling of cooperation or belonging, and children are left wondering, "Who is in charge here?"

3. Authoritative Style (The Active Parent). Active parenting is, in some respects, a balance between the autocratic and permissive methods, but it is much more. In an active parenting household, parents and children have rights and responsibilities. The parent is the leader and encourages cooperation and stimulates learning. There is order and routine, and every person in the family is an important member.

Understanding Behavior: Purpose Not Cause

We should ask ourselves, "What is the purpose or goal of their behavior? What payoff is their behavior aimed at getting?"

In order to understand another person's behavior, it does little good to look back and try to figure out what caused the behavior. There are so many factors influencing behavior that it is virtually impossible to pinpoint them all. More important yet, humans are beings with free will. We choose how to behave based on our experience, values, and goals for the future. So to understand why people, including children, behave the way they do, we should ask ourselves, "What is the purpose or goal of their behavior? What payoff is their behavior aimed at getting?"

For example, 6-year-old Alina refused to clean up her mess in the family room after her father had told her to. Her father was angry and threatened to take away TV for a week. Alina stormed out of the room saying, "It's not fair!"

Why has Alina refused to comply with her father's order? What is her purpose or goal? Does her behavior get her the payoff she wants? To answer these questions, we want to look at four basic goals of all children's behavior, and then see which one Alina might achieve through her behavior.

Four Goals of Child Behavior

In Chapter One we said that the purpose of parenting is to protect and prepare our children to survive and to thrive in the kind of society in which they will live. Building on the foundation laid by Rudolf Dreikurs, there are four goals that enable humans to survive and thrive. These same four goals govern our children's behavior:

- **contact/belonging**

- **power**

- **protection**

- **withdrawal**

Let's look at each of these goals more closely, particularly as they appear during the years of childhood.

Contact/Belonging

The basic need of every human being is to belong. A baby could not survive without others to depend upon. Neither could the human species have survived throughout history without belonging to various groups: clans, families, communities, cities, states, and nations, to name a few.

Out of this desire to belong, each of us develops the goal of making contact—physical or emotional—with other human beings. For an infant, the need to be held is actually critical to its survival. Later, contact with Mom and Dad helps the growing child develop a sense of belonging in the family. The self-esteem and courage that grow out of this belonging make it possible for the child to make positive contact outside the family. Schools, religious organizations, sports leagues, and other institutions offer additional opportunities for contact and belonging.

Power

We want to empower our children to develop their talents and skills.

Each one of us wants to influence our environment and gain at least a measure of control. We would like for things to go our way; we want the power to make that happen. It is through learning that we become able to do this. As the saying goes, "Knowledge is power." As parents, we want to empower our children to develop their talents and skills and become competent individuals who contribute to the common good.

Protection

To survive and thrive we must be able to protect ourselves, our families and our nation. Our instinct to repel attacks—whether physical or psychological—has led to the development of elaborate systems of justice and defense. Children will also look for ways to protect themselves from physical harm or from threats to their self-esteem. But because they lack a mature understanding of justice and the interconnectedness of people, they often strike out in ways that are unproductive and even harmful. Parents and teachers can help children learn responsible methods of protection while at the same time using our adult resources to offer safe environments for them.

Withdrawal

Time-outs are essential and refreshing in any sport. Just as a child seeks contact, at other times he needs to withdraw, regroup, center. Withdrawal is a kind of counterbalancing act to the goal of belonging. Our early survival instinct has also taught us to withdraw from danger.

Positive and Negative Approaches to the Four Goals

An interesting aspect of these four basic goals is that they may be approached through either positive or negative behavior. Active Parenting Now has the philosophy that there are no good or bad children, only those who choose to pursue these four basic goals in either positive or negative ways. Children with high self-esteem and courage will generally choose the positive approaches. Those with low self-esteem who are discouraged will more likely choose the negative approaches. The following chart provides some labels we can use to distinguish these approaches:

Child's Goal	Positive Approach	Negative Approach
Contact/Belonging	Contributing Cooperating	Undue Attention-Seeking
Power	Independence Competence	Rebellion
Protection	Assertiveness Promoting justice Forgiveness	Revenge
Withdrawal	Appropriate Avoidance	Undue Avoidance

The Parent-Child Cycle

Since the parent's behavior is the event that often triggers the child's thinking, and the child's behavior is the event that triggers the parent's thinking, we can merge the two together and diagram a parent–child interaction like this:

The Parent-Child Cycle

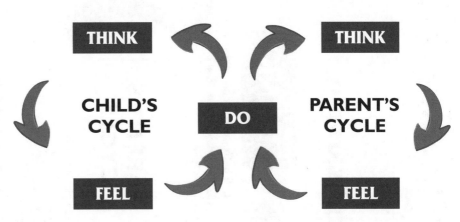

The interaction goes around and around in the universal symbol for "infinity."

Notice that since behavior is how we influence each other, the "do" becomes the triggering "event" for the other person's "think-feel-do" cycle.

The interaction goes around and around in the universal symbol for "infinity." Unless one side does the unexpected to change the interaction, the cycle continues until parent and child physically separate…and then resumes later with a new triggering event.

The arrows coming out of the "do" box on each side not only trigger the thinking of the other person's cycle, but also feeds back to our own thinking. This represents the fact that we evaluate our own behavior according to our values and how well we think the behavior is working to accomplish our goals. We choose to continue our behavior or make changes based on our interpretation of the experience.

Let's look at an example that illustrates how the parent-child cycle works. Looking at the chart on the next page, start with number one under the child's thinking. Then, remembering that thinking is often unconscious, follow the numbers throughout the cycle between the child and the parent to see an example of a child pursuing undue attention at the dinner table, ending at step 15.

The Parent–Child Cycle Example

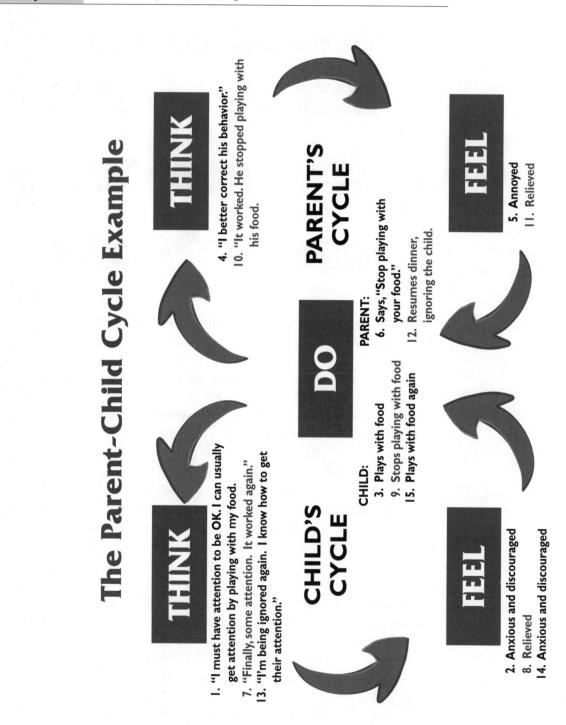

THINK

4. "I better correct his behavior."
10. "It worked. He stopped playing with his food.

PARENT'S CYCLE

FEEL

5. Annoyed
11. Relieved

DO

PARENT:

6. Says, "Stop playing with your food."
12. Resumes dinner, ignoring the child.

THINK

1. "I must have attention to be OK. I can usually get attention by playing with my food.
7. "Finally, some attention. It worked again."
13. "I'm being ignored again. I know how to get their attention."

CHILD'S CYCLE

CHILD:

3. Plays with food
9. Stops playing with food
15. Plays with food again

FEEL

2. Anxious and discouraged
8. Relieved
14. Anxious and discouraged

What can the parent do to avoid paying off the misbehavior and to break the cycle?

In the case of undue attention-seeking, we want to act more and talk less. The discipline that works best is either a brief confrontation through an "I" message or a logical consequence.

For example:

> *"Either stop playing with your food or you will need to leave the table. You decide."*

This logical consequence does give the child some brief attention. However, if the child resumes playing with his food, the parent then follows through with the consequence.

For example:

> *"I see you have decided to leave the table tonight. Please put your plate in the sink and we will try again tomorrow."*

Now, the child must deal with the consequence of getting no attention at all, which spoils his pay-off and breaks the cycle. Remember however that kids will test to see if we will be consistent with our new approach, so this parent should expect more undue attention-getting behaviors in other areas at least for a while.

Note: If the child refuses to leave the table, she is moving into the negative approach of rebellion. We'll cover this approach next.

Remember, too, that discipline is only half of the process for redirecting misbehavior. Discipline is designed to limit the negative behavior. However it is just as important to actively encourage the child toward the positive approach. In the case of undue attention seeking, we want to help the child achieve the recognition and contact he wants by playing a useful role. We can help find meaningful ways for the child to contribute to the family while ignoring some of the unproductive attention-getting behaviors. Using the encouragement skills we will learn in Chapter Five will help.

How To Determine a Child's Goal

Because parents do not usually know the goals behind a child's misbehavior, we often take an action that makes the problem worse. In other words, our discipline actually pays off her negative behavior by helping the child achieve her goal. And if negative behavior works, why not continue to use it? After all, it's usually the easier approach.

The first step, then, is to determine what your child really wants. Once we know the goal, we can help redirect the child to choose a positive approach to getting it. This requires some detective work on our part. There are two clues that will usually tell us the child's goal:

There are two clues that will usually tell us the child's goal: our own feeling during a conflict and the child's response to our attempts at correcting the misbehavior.

1. **Our own feeling during a conflict.** Are we annoyed, angry, hurt or helpless? Because much of our child's misbehavior is aimed at us, becoming aware of our own feelings during a conflict can be a powerful clue to his goals.

2. **The child's response to our attempts at correcting the misbehavior.** How does a child behave after we have made an effort to correct the misbehavior?

The chart on the following page is a guide for using this information:

If we feel...	And the child's response to correction is to...	Then the negative approach is...	To the child's goal of...
Annoyed	Stop the behavior, but start again very soon	Undue Attention-Seeking	Contact/Belonging
Angry	Increase the misbehavior or give in only to fight again another day	Rebellion	Power
Hurt	Continue to hurt us or increase the misbehavior	Revenge	Protection
Helpless	Become passive; refuse to try	Undue Avoidance	Withdrawal

Let's look more closely at each of the four negative approaches.

1. Undue Attention-Seeking

Some children find ways to keep people busy with them.

The child who seeks contact through undue attention-seeking probably has the mistaken belief that she must be the center of attention in order to belong. While young children will do things to get this attention from their parents, older children prefer the attention of peers. They may become class clowns or the ones who are constantly in trouble—anything to stay in the limelight.

Such children find ways to keep people busy with them. An undue attention-seeking child may act forgetful, or helpless, or lazy, putting the parent in his service with reminders and coaxing. Or the child may get attention by clowning, asking constant questions, pestering, or making a nuisance of himself. He may even resort to positive behavior, but only so far as there is a parent to watch. When the parent hears, "Look at this, Mommy," over and over again, even positive behavior can be for the wrong purpose. Adults typically feel annoyed or irritated. When we correct the child, he will usually stop the misbehavior. After all, our correction has given the attention the child seeks. However, the child will usually want more contact soon, and will resume the misbehavior.

How parents pay off the negative approach of undue attention-seeking. We tend to remind, nag, coax, complain, give mini-lectures, scold, and otherwise stay in contact with the child. This attention is the payoff that reinforces the child's mistaken approach to achieving contact. After all, to such children, even negative attention is better than no attention.

What can parents do differently? The key to helping your child shift from the negative to the positive approach with any of the four goals is to do the unexpected. We have to break the pattern the child has come to expect, avoiding the payoffs that maintain their mistaken ideas. To see this more clearly, let's revisit the parent-child cycle that we introduced in Chapter Three:

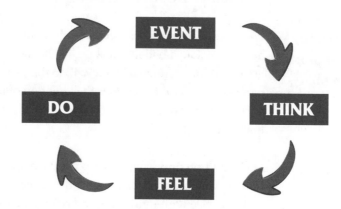

Remember that children respond to events in their lives in the order of the arrows: First, their thinking is triggered, including unconscious beliefs, attitudes, and values. This produces a feeling, and together the thinking and feeling produce a response. In the case of misbehavior, the child's thinking involves a negative approach to one of the four goals. For example, with undue attention-seeking as the negative approach to the goal of belonging, the child might be unconsciously thinking, "I must have Mommy's attention to be okay." This low self-esteem belief produces a feeling of anxiety and discouragement. To eliminate these unpleasant feelings, the child chooses an annoying behavior that in the past has served to gain her mother's attention. If the mother continues, as expected, to remind, nag, lecture, or correct, the child will think, "Yes, she notices me again and I am okay." She will feel temporarily better, but soon will want another dose of undue attention.

2. Rebellion

Of the four negative approaches, rebellion is the most common and creates the most distress in families and schools. The child who becomes discouraged trying to achieve his goal of power in a positive way can easily find power in the negative approach of rebellion. He does this by trying to boss others around or by showing them that they can't boss him. After all, the ability to say "no" is very powerful…as every two-year-old quickly learns. In fact, one of the rules of power is this:

The person in position to say "no" is in the more powerful position.

The child who becomes discouraged trying to achieve his goal of power in a positive way can easily find power in the negative approach of rebellion.

This is why power struggles are so frustrating for parents. We are bigger, smarter, more experienced and have the authority to decide what's in the best interest of our families—but even so, we cannot make our children do what we want. They have the free will to choose, and if they choose to resist us, our frustration can easily turn to anger. This feeling of anger is the major clue that you are in a power struggle and that your child has chosen a rebellious approach to his goal of power. The other clue is that power-driven children are very persistent and often respond to correction by continuing the

misbehavior, often in open defiance. For example: "No! You can't make me!" We'll cover some tips for avoiding this type of power struggle later in this chapter.

How parents pay off the negative approach of rebellion. Parents who tend towards the dictator style often fight fire with fire. Words such as, "No, you can't make me!" are fighting words to an autocratic parent. It hooks their own desire for power by triggering thoughts such as, "I've got to be in control here; I'm the parent!" and of course, "Oh yes I can!" They meet the child's challenge with a show of force and wind up fighting, either verbally or with punishment. Ironically, the more you fight with a child over power, the more she perceives that she is winning. After all, even if she eventually does what you want, say after a spanking or other punishment, she still has the secondary payoff of knowing that she made you angry. This in itself is very powerful and acts to reinforce the parent-child cycle. "Look how powerful my rebellion makes me. I made Daddy so mad!"

Parents who tend towards the doormat style often make the mistake of giving in to rebellious children. These parents want to avoid confrontation and give in to the child's unreasonable demands and refusals. The pay-off is that the child gets her own way. "Look how powerful I am. I made Daddy give in!"

To successfully side-step the struggle for power, we must refuse to fight or give in.

What can parents do differently? To successfully side-step the struggle for power, we must refuse to fight or give in. The parent who tends toward the dictator style can communicate more confidence in the child's ability to make decisions by himself. Rather than boss, we can give a choice. We can let the child make some mistakes, and then experience the consequences...without our lecturing or humiliating. We can set up family council meetings (Chapter Six) to involve the child in making decisions that affect the whole family. We can use the family enrichment activities, communication skills, and methods of encouragement described in this program to begin winning a more cooperative relationship. And most important, we can show the child that we are not interested in fighting. Instead, we will work together to find solutions, and when discipline is necessary, we will use logical consequences rather than anger and punishment.

3. Revenge

Revenge is one of the oldest and most primitive motivations for human behavior. Unfortunately, it is also one of the most counterproductive. It grows out of the goal of protection. "You hurt me and if I hurt you back, then you'll think twice before hurting me again," seems to be the thinking that produces this behavior. And because revenge does often work as a deterrent, it continues to exist on both large and small scales. The problem is that more often than not, revenge leads to more revenge in an ever-escalating cycle of hurt and retaliation.

This escalation can be seen in the violence of our own society. Students and adults alike often take revenge for real or imagined injustices by shooting fellow students, workers, or even strangers. While kids with high self-esteem and courage are able to pursue their goal of protection through assertiveness (standing up for themselves), justice (using legal channels to address their grievances) and forgiveness (clearing the slate so that neither side feels the need to retaliate), those with lower self-esteem and courage more often resort to revenge.

In the family, we often see how an increase in a power struggle can easily lead to the negative approach of revenge, especially if the child feels that the parent has "won too many battles," or has hurt the child in the process. The child decides that the best form of protection is to hurt back. And while this seldom results in physical violence, the child still has ways to inflict hurt upon the parent. In fact, it is this feeling of hurt that is the clue that the child is pursuing revenge. And because our autocratic parenting tradition tells us that when children hurt us we should punish them more, an escalating revenge cycle begins.

Because parents want to see their children survive and thrive, they can never win this revenge war. All children have to do to hurt parents is fail. They can fail at school; they can fail with peers; they can fail with drugs, with sex, and, ultimately, they can fail at life by committing suicide. The result each time is a parent left hurting.

How parents pay off the negative approach of revenge. When children seek to protect themselves by getting revenge, they are usually feeling very discouraged. When we retaliate with punishment and put-downs, we discourage them further and confirm their belief that they have a right to hurt us back. The more we hurt them, the more they want to hurt us back.

By refusing to hurt back, we can do the unexpected and break the cycle.

What can parents do differently? Someone has to stop the revenge cycle if the situation is to improve. We can stubbornly demand that the child change (which is what many of us have been taught to do), or we can play the leadership role in the family and call a cease-fire. By refusing to hurt back, we can do the unexpected and break the cycle. As with a power struggle, this does not mean giving in to unreasonable demands. It means that we remain firm, yet loving.

It will help us to remember that no child is born "bad" or "mean." For children to act this way, they have to be hurting inside. The first step, then, is to do what we can to stop whatever is hurting the child. If it is our behavior, then we can take a new approach. If someone else is hurting her, we can use active communication to support the child in handling it herself. If more direct action is called for, we can intervene or get outside help.

Sometimes, however, the child has not been wronged but is hurting because of her misconception about how life ought to work. Perhaps we have coddled the child in the past, and now we have begun to treat him (and ourselves) more respectfully. In these cases a calm and firm manner will help. Finally, the skills discussed for handling a power struggle, especially those for building a positive relationship and the FLAC method, will also be useful in redirecting a revenge-seeking child.

4. Undue Avoidance

Children who become extremely discouraged may sink so low in their own self-esteem that they give up trying. Their belief becomes "I can't succeed so I'll avoid trying; then I can't fail." They develop an apathy and lack of motivation that often leaves parents and educators feeling helpless. Such children may become truant from school, fail to do assignments, and avoid peers. In the teen years, tobacco, alcohol, and other drugs may become a way for them to avoid the challenges of life as they find temporary relief from their own discouragement.

How parents pay off the negative approach of undue avoidance. It is often our own perfectionism that causes the child's long slow slide into undue avoidance. When we focus excessively on mistakes, when nothing ever seems to be good enough for us, when all we talk about is his great "potential," the child may give up trying altogether.

Once a child has chosen avoidance, we often make the mistake of giving up on him. We write him off as a "loser" and stop making an effort to help. Or we yell and scream, humiliate and punish. Either way, we send the message: "You're not good enough for us." This confirms the child's own evaluation of himself, and justifies his avoidance.

Practice patience and give a lot of encouragement.

What can parents do differently? Communicate to the child that whether she succeeds or fails, our love is unconditional. In addition to such acceptance of the child, we will need to practice patience and give a lot of encouragement. We can remind ourselves that the child is exaggerating her avoidance to see if the worst is true (that she really is as bad off as she thinks). We can help the child find tasks that she can perform successfully, so that she can begin to break the misconception of herself as a loser. And we can help her to see that mistakes are for learning, and failure is just a lesson on the road to success.

The chart on the following page summarizes our understanding of children's behavior:

Basic Goal of Child's Action	Child's Positive or Negative Approach to Goal	Child's Belief	Parent's Typical Feeling	Child's Response	How to Redirect
Contact/ Belonging	Recognition	My contributions are recognized. I belong by cooperating. I enjoy human contact.	Closeness	Cooperation and contribution	Encourage cooperation, acknowledge the child's contributions.
	Undue Attention-Seeking	I belong only when I'm noticed or served. The world must revolve around me.	Annoyance	Stops, but begins again very soon	Ignore the behavior. Give the child full attention at other times. Use logical and natural consequences; act, don't talk.
Power	Independence	I am able to influence what happens to me. I am responsible for my life.	Admiration	Responsible, self-motivated behavior, learning	Give responsibilities. Continue to encourage.
	Rebellion	I belong only when I'm the boss or when I'm showing you that you can't boss me.	Anger	Escalates behavior or gives in only to fight again another day.	Remove yourself from the conflict. Talk about it after a cooling-off period. Don't fight or give in. Use FLAC Method.
Protection	Assertiveness, Justice, Forgiveness	When attacked or treated unfairly, I can stand up for myself and those I love. I am able to forgive and even contribute to those who have wronged me.	Love	Positive contact	Express your own positive feelings; demonstrate assertiveness and forgiveness in your own relationships.
	Revenge	I've been hurt and will get even by huritng back. Then maybe they'll learn they can't get away with huriting me.	Hurt	To continue to hurt, or escalate misbehavior	Refuse to be hurt. Withdraw from the conflict. Show love to vengeful child. Avoid temptation to hurt back. Use FLAC Method.
Withdrawal	Centering	There are times when I need to be alone. And there are situations to be left alone.	Respect	Resumes contact when ready	Respect the child's wishes to be alone. Don't press. Later, use active communication.
	Avoidance	I'm a failure at everything. Leave me alone. Expect nothing from me.	Helplessness	Becomes passive; refuses to try; gives up	Be patient; find ways to encourage child. Build skills using baby steps.

Avoiding Power Struggles

The secret to avoiding a power struggle is to neither fight nor give in.

Remember, as soon as you get angry, you lose the power struggle.

This is not an easy task, but with a little parent "judo" it can be accomplished. While autocratic parents tend to fight head on with a challenging child, Judo is the art of sidestepping the opponent's attack, and using his own thrust to throw him off balance. By doing the unexpected and not fighting, yet not giving in, a parent can influence the child to change some of the thinking that drives the parent-child cycle. This requires first that we stay calm and do not take rebellion personally. (See the section on "managing anger" at the end of this chapter.) Remember, as soon as you get angry, you lose the power struggle.

We can also "do the unexpected" and communicate more confidence in the child's ability to make decisions by himself. Rather than boss, we can give choices. We can let the child make some mistakes, and then experience the consequences ... without lecturing or humiliating. We can set up family meetings to involve the child in making decisions that affect the whole family. We can use the Family Enrichment Activities, communication skills, and methods of encouragement described in this program to begin winning a more cooperative relationship. And, most important, we can show the child that we are not interested in fighting. Instead, we will work together to find solutions, and when discipline is necessary, we will use logical consequences rather than anger and punishment.

The parent who tends toward the doormat style, in addition to using the Active Parenting skills just described, can refuse to give in to the child's unreasonable demands. We can stop being short-order cooks, clean-up services, wake-up callers, and last-minute chauffeurs. We can set firm limits, negotiate within those limits, refuse to be intimidated by displays of anger, and enforce the consequences of breaking the limits. We can let our children know that while we believe they should be treated respectfully, we expect to be treated respectfully as well.

Let's see how a number of Active Parenting skills can be combined to reduce the "flack" experienced in a power struggle.

The FLAC Method

The acronym, FLAC, can help you remember how to defuse a power struggle without fighting or giving in. The letters stand for:

Feelings

Limits

Alternatives

Consequences

Let's use the following situation as an example. Nine-year-old Justin , is angry about going to bed and keeps getting up for one thing after another. His father is about to get very angry when he remembers that getting angry and shouting at Justin is what his son expects and will only fuel the power struggle between them. Instead, he does the unexpected and sits down on his son's bed and says:

Father: *I guess I really don't blame you for wanting to stay up later, Justin. I never liked going to bed, either. It feels like you're missing out on something.* (F for Feelings)

Justin: *(Surprised at his father's empathy) Yeah.*

Father: *Still, we all need our sleep to stay healthy and function well the next day, so you can't just stay up until you crash.* (L for Limits)

Justin: *But I don't want to go to bed now. It's too early.*

Father: *Hmm, well maybe there's an alternative. I might be willing to let you stay up an extra half hour if you were to use it as quiet time to relax yourself. Say, maybe by reading in bed.* **(A for Alternative)**

Justin: *Can I read fun stuff or does it have to be a schoolbook?*

Father: *You can read fun stuff. But here's the deal. If you are tired the next day or don't get up on time, or if you get out of bed after the half hour is up, then you have to go to bed on time the next night with no reading or hassle. Agreed?* **(C for Consequences)**

Justin: *Ok.*

Let's review the four steps:

Feelings. We saw in Chapter Two how important it is to listen and respond to our children's feelings. When we show empathy for their feelings about the situation, we suddenly move from being the enemy to being on their side in finding a solution to a common problem. This goes a long way towards defusing the power struggle ("don't fight") while laying the groundwork for a win-win solution.

Limits. By reminding his son of the limits of the situation and providing a good reason for the limits, dad defines the problem to be solved ("don't give in"). It's much less provocative to say, "because the situation calls for this," rather than, "because I said so." In this case, the situation calls for a good night's sleep.

By negotiating within reasonable limits, we can often make the limits more palatable for our children.

Alternatives. Once people disengage from a struggle for power, you'd be surprised how often an acceptable alternative can be found. There is no magic number of minutes every child needs to sleep. The extra 30 minutes is unlikely to cause a problem, and it has the additional benefit of encouraging the importance of reading. By negotiating within reasonable limits, we can often make the limits more palatable for our children. Even when the limits are firm, you can often find an alternative within those limits that makes it more acceptable to the child.

Consequences. Some writers suggest that consequences only make matters worse with a rebellious child. Others suggest coming down even harder in a display of "tough love." However, if you can avoid getting angry (which turns the logical consequence into a punishment) then consequences can be useful as one more tool in motivating the child to live within the limits. They do not need to be harsh, just enough to remind the child that they are responsible for their actions.

Parenting and Anger

Children and adults who cannot control their temper create pain for themselves and those around them.

The management of anger has become recognized in recent years as vitally important to families and throughout society. Anger that turns to rage and then to violence creates headlines that range from school shootings and terrorist attacks to family violence. Even on smaller scales, children and adults who cannot control their temper create pain for themselves and those around them. Yet anger is also a natural part of life, so we are not quite sure what to make of this complicated emotion. Perhaps these pages will give you a new view of an old subject.

As you read, keep in mind the "think-feel-do" cycle.

The Anatomy of Anger

Response to frustration. Anger is an emotional and physiological response to frustration. If an important need, want, or desire is blocked for us, our bodies and emotions react with intense feelings that we often label as anger.

For example, a caveman walking through the woods comes upon a fallen tree that blocks his path. On the other side of the tree are some berries he wants to pick and eat. He strains to push the fallen tree aside, but he isn't strong enough, and he becomes frustrated at the thought of not reaching his goal. His frustration produces physiological changes in his body that enable him to lift the fallen tree savagely and hurl it aside.

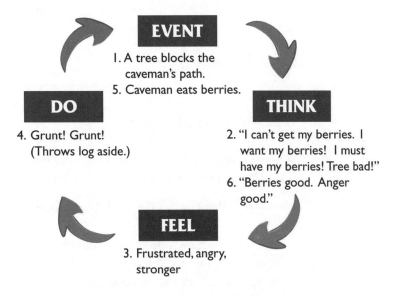

EVENT

1. A tree blocks the caveman's path.
5. Caveman eats berries.

THINK

2. "I can't get my berries. I want my berries! I must have my berries! Tree bad!"
6. "Berries good. Anger good."

FEEL

3. Frustrated, angry, stronger

DO

4. Grunt! Grunt! (Throws log aside.)

Purpose of anger. Anger releases certain chemicals into our bloodstream. These chemicals produce changes that make us stronger, faster, and look intimidating. This is known as the "fight/flight" syndrome, because it makes us ready to fight danger or run from it. In primitive times, the added power it produced helped us survive when problems were settled by brute force.

Old brain/new brain theory. Anger is associated with the so-called "old brain," which has been present in human beings since the beginning of our existence. But as the "new brain" has evolved around the old brain, so has human intelligence and societies based on law. This gives us the ability to handle problems with solutions other than brute force.

"Use," not "lose," our temper. However, even in modern societies, anger sometimes pays off. Rudolf Dreikurs once said that people do not "lose" their temper; they "use" their temper. What he meant was that people some-

123

times use anger to intimidate others into giving them what they want. Since anger is often accompanied by violence, this intimidation can sometimes be effective. But it carries a heavy price. Anger used to bully damages relationships and is hurtful. Worse yet, it can lead to violent behavior and crime.

How To Use Anger Positively

The Message of Anger

Our own angry feelings tell us that one of our goals is being blocked. It clearly sends this message:

"Act! Don't just sit there; get up and do something!"

If we do something soon, we can often solve the problem before it gets worse, and before we "blow up." If we don't act but try to ignore the message, several things could happen:

1. The problem might go away by other means, but this is a risky and uncertain possibility.

2. Our anger may grow in intensity until it propels us into some action, which is likely to be desperate, unthinking, and potentially violent.

3. Our anger will seethe internally, expressing itself in unexpected ways: headaches, rashes, ulcers—even heart attacks.

How to Act on Anger

There are a number of useful ways to listen to the message of anger and take positive action:

1. Act to change the situation. (Do something different.) Struggle until you remove the fallen tree.

Example:

> *Use effective discipline skills such as "I" messages, logical consequences, and The FLAC method.*

2. Reduce the importance of the goal. Put it in perspective. Think something different.

Examples:

> *Although you may want the berries very much, be aware that you don't need them for your survival.*
>
> *Your child refuses to take a bath. Remind yourself that your goal of a daily bath is less important than your good relationship with your child and that missing a bath will not seriously affect your child.*

3. Change your goals. Find an alternative. Again, think something different.

Examples:

> *Decide that the berries are not the only solution to the hunger problem and look for an alternative—maybe an apple tree near the river.*
>
> *Give up your goal of having your child play the piano and encourage an alternative activity of her choice.*

Helping Children Use Their Anger

Teach children that violence is not an okay way to solve problems.

Because children are usually more primitive in their expression of emotions, they will often resemble the caveman when experiencing frustration and anger. Tantrums and hitting are fairly common with young children. However, it is increasingly important in these days of "zero tolerance" for aggressive behavior that we teach

children that violence is not an okay way to solve problems. There are several ways parents can help:

1. Give them a good model. The way you handle your own problems and frustrations will provide a model for your children.

- *Do you fly into a rage, hurling insults and humiliating remarks?*
- *Do you strike out at others?*
- *Do you sink into a depression (an adult temper tantrum or "silent storm")?*

2. Guide them with words to find more effective forms of expression.

Examples:

"You have the right to feel the way you do, but in our family, we don't scream and blame; we look for solutions."

"I can see that you are angry. Can you tell me with words instead of hitting?"

"When you get angry at me, please tell me without calling me names. I don't call you names; please don't call me names."

"Take your sails out of their wind."

3. Remove yourself from a power struggle. When children have tantrums, you can acknowledge their anger, but at the same time "take your sails out of their wind." Don't try to overpower the child; withdraw instead. This action says to the child, "I am not intimidated by your show of temper and will not give in, but I won't punish or humiliate you either." The result is that children who get neither a fight nor their own way after throwing tantrums will usually find more acceptable ways to influence people. If you need a quiet place to withdraw from the power struggle, try the bathroom. It's the one place where a little privacy is usually expected.

4. Use the FLAC Method. In those situations where a child's tantrum interferes with the rights of others (like in a restaurant, or when company is in the home), you can acknowledge the child's feeling, remind him of the limits, offer an alternative, and follow through with logical consequences.

For example:

> *I know you are angry about having to go shopping with me, and I'll admit that it isn't much fun. Still, we do want to eat dinner tonight so we need to get this done. How about if you help me out by putting the food in the cart? That will make it go faster and then you can help me pick out some of your favorite desserts.*

If the child continues to act out his anger, add a logical consequence:

> *Dennis, you can either calm down and help me shop or we will have to go sit in the car until you can, then we definitely won't have time to stop by the park.*

Children must learn that there are consequences for violent and aggressive behavior.

Children must learn that there are consequences for violent and aggressive behavior. The child who acts out his anger by breaking something can help pay for its replacement. The child who hits or bullies can be removed from other kids for a period of time to think about how he can make it up to the other person. As with all logical consequences, stay calm and firm when delivering them. Your goal is not to hurt the child, which may just begin a revenge cycle, but rather to teach him.

5. Allow your child to influence your decisions. When a person feels powerless to influence leaders, frustration gives way to anger and rebellion. If you allow your child to influence your decisions concerning her, she will not be as likely to resort to such unconscious tactics as bedwetting, soiling, and stomach disorders, to name a few.

The method your child uses to influence your decisions will be influenced by what you allow to work. If you "give in" to tantrums, whining, or tears, the child will learn to use these tactics again. If you redirect your child to express his anger respectfully, listen to his arguments, and sometimes change your decisions, then your child learns the important skill of negotiation.

Family Meeting: "Active Problem Solving"

We've learned that as parents we need to teach our children to negotiate solutions to problems within limits that are acceptable for the situation. This can go a long way towards increasing harmony in families and preparing kids to succeed in our democratic society. "Active Problem Solving" is a simple five-step model for negotiating problems as a family. We have seen elements of these steps in many of the skills we have already covered, including problem prevention talks and the FLAC Method. However, applying them as a family in a meeting has the added value of communicating that "We are a family of problem solvers where everyone's ideas and feelings are valuable." The participation and respect generated can lessen power struggles while generating a cooperative energy that produces highly creative solutions to problems. Do not feel that you have to use these guidelines rigidly, but use them as aids to hold your meetings.

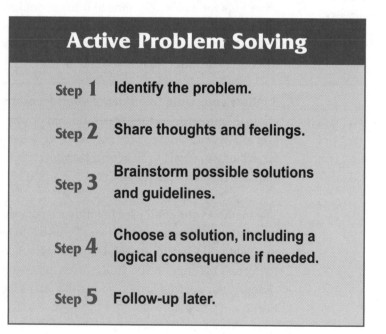

Active Problem Solving

Step 1 Identify the problem.

Step 2 Share thoughts and feelings.

Step 3 Brainstorm possible solutions and guidelines.

Step 4 Choose a solution, including a logical consequence if needed.

Step 5 Follow-up later.

Step 1. Identify the problem.

It is important to begin by stating the problem in terms of behavior and not by attacking your child's personality.

Poor:

> *I have a problem with your being lazy.*

Better:

> *I have a problem with how messy your room is.*

Step 2. Share thoughts and feelings.

Remembering that building our children's emotional intelligence means helping them learn to listen to other people's thoughts and feelings as well as their own, the next step is to encourage sharing. Use the skills we learned in Chapter Two to avoid communication blocks while getting everyone's thoughts and feelings on the table.

Child: *But it's my room so what's the big deal?*

Mother: *I understand it's your room, and that putting things away is a hassle. But I guess I've learned how important it is to be organized and I want you to be able to find things when you need them.*

Father: *And I just feel kind of frustrated when I walk in there and clothes are lying everywhere, drawers half open, and toys all over the place.*

Child: *Good, then don't go in there.*

Father: *Well, I don't feel good about not helping you learn good habits. Besides, in our family we want to take pride in our home, and that means keeping it reasonably neat.*

Step 3. Brainstorm possible solutions and guidelines.

By generating possible solutions and discussing them as you go you can often come up with something everybody can live with. This is called "consensus" decision making. You don't vote, but rather continue to discuss until you find an agreement that everyone can accept. When a consensus cannot be reached, then it is up to the parents as leaders in the family to decide the best of the possible choices, taking into account everyone's thoughts and feelings.

Mother: *Maybe we can think of a solution that everyone feels good about. Anybody have an idea?*

After discussion...

Mother: *Okay, then we agree that we won't bug you every day about cleaning your room, but you will take care of it before you go play outside on Saturdays. I'll help you organize it this Saturday so that you'll know what we expect from now on. Oh, and we all liked dad's idea of taking a picture of it afterwards so you'll have a model of what it should look like before you have us come check it each week.*

Step 4. Choose a solution with a logical consequence as necessary.

In our example about the messy room, the family came up with a solution and logical consequence in Step 3 as part of their brainstorming. However, there will be situations where a logical consequence is added after the solution is chosen in order to motivate the child to keep the agreement. Whether you need a consequence or not depends on your child's track record. If he has been responsible about keeping his agreements, then adding a logical consequence might be seen as disrespectful and may actually backfire. However, with other kids, they will understand the need to add a consequence.

Step 5. Follow-up later.

There is an old saying that "you get what you inspect, not what you expect." In other words, we need to expend the effort to make sure agreements are kept and that consequences are followed through. If the child has kept his agreement, it is essential that you encourage her with a word of praise or even a positive "I" Message as described in Chapter Three.

Child: *Okay…I'm ready for somebody to check my room.*

Father: *Okay…nice job. Let's just check the picture…very nice. Everything seems to be in place and I especially like the way you put your toy lion on the pillow. That's a creative touch. Your room really looks great.*

Of course if there are still problems, you can compliment the progress and still remind about what needs to be completed.

Father: *Say, this is really starting to look good. I like the way you've organized things. Let's see how the picture looked about making the bed…*

Child: *Oh, yeah…I'll fix it.*

Father: *Great. Then you'll be all set to go outside and play.*

Ground Rules for Conducting Problem-Solving Discussions

Every person has an equal voice. Although it is hard for parents to give up some of their authority, problem-solving discussions don't work well unless every person has an equal voice in the decisions made. Every person, including small children, needs to feel that he will be heard and can make a difference in what the family decides to do. Children will not be very enthusiastic about family meetings, nor will they derive much benefit from them, if the meetings are merely forums for parents to decide what everybody will do.

Everyone may share what she thinks and feels about each issue. It is important that every person at family meetings be encouraged to speak up and say what she thinks and feels about whatever question is on the table. In order to make decisions that are reasonable and fair to everyone, the family needs to hear everyone's opinions and feelings, even the negative ones.

Decisions are made by consensus. Reaching a consensus means that when there is disagreement, the parties involved discuss the matter until everyone agrees. It does not mean a vote is taken and the majority rules. If an agreement cannot be reached in the meeting, then one of two things may happen: either the matter is tabled until the next meeting when it will be discussed further, or (if it urgently requires decision and action) the parent may exercise his duty as head of the household to make a decision and carry it out.

All decisions are in effect until the next meeting. Whatever decisions are made at a problem-solving discussion, they should be carried out at least until the next meeting, when they can be discussed again. Complaints after the meeting about decisions made should always bring this answer: "Bring it up again at the next meeting."

Some decisions are reserved for parents to make. Meeting together does not imply that the parents must always do whatever the children decide to do. Basic questions of health and welfare are parental responsibilities, and the decision is sometimes theirs alone to make. But discussion should always be allowed and encouraged. Sometimes when a parent has been told by her company that a move is required, she can't ask the children for approval. However, the parent can allow them to express their thoughts, concerns and feelings about the move, and to share in the planning.

Family Enrichment Activity: Teaching Skills

Teaching your child a skill empowers her in a very positive way and enriches your relationship with her.

Part of developing self-esteem and courage is seeing oneself as a capable individual. When you take the time to teach your child a skill, you not only help her become more capable, you also give her positive ways of achieving the goal of power. In fact, teaching your child a skill empowers her in a very positive way and enriches your relationship with her.

The following steps can help you teach a skill effectively:

1. **Motivate.** Encourage your child to want to learn the skill by explaining the value it has to the child or the entire family. For example:

   "Once you learn how to make your own sandwich for lunch, you won't always have to wait for me. Maybe sometimes you could even help me make lunch for everyone."

2. **Select a good time.** Pick a time when neither you nor your child will be rushed or upset by other things.

3. **Break the skill down into baby steps.** When skills are learned one step at a time, there are more successes to help build courage and motivation. For example:

   "The first step is to get all of the ingredients out on the counter: the bread, the peanut butter, the honey, and a knife."

4. **Demonstrate.** Show your child how to perform the skill, explaining slowly as you do. For example:

   "Next, watch how I dip the knife into the peanut butter, then slowly spread it onto a piece of bread."

5. Let your child try. Let your child perform the skill while you stand by, ready to offer help if he needs it. Be gentle about mistakes, and let it be fun. For example:

"Okay, now you try it. Just dip the knife in the jar so that you get plenty of that yummy peanut butter on it."

6. Encourage, encourage, encourage. Make plenty of encouraging comments that acknowledge your child's efforts and results. This builds self-esteem and keeps his motivation high to continue learning. For example:

"Great! That's the way to do it."

7. Work or play together. Once your child has learned the skill, you can sometimes work or play together, so that you can both enjoy the companionship of the activity. For example:

"Let's eat!"

Chapter 4

HOME ACTIVITIES

- Use your understanding of the four goals of child behavior to avoid "paying-off" a misbehavior, then use the **FLAC** method, or other discipline approach that we have learned, to redirect the chid to a positive approach. Complete the worksheet on page 211.

- Have a Family Meeting using Active Problem Solving to address a problem your family is facing. Complete the worksheet on page 212.

- Family Enrichment Activity: Teach a skill (or be taught one). Complete the worksheet on page 213.

- Continue to "take care of the caregiver, and add to your chart on page 195.

Building Courage, Character, and Self-Esteem

A long time ago, before the advent of convenience stores, there was a group of humans called "milkmen." There was also a 5-year-old boy who was afraid of the dark. Early one morning before the sun had risen, his mother, hoping to help her child overcome his fear, encouraged the little boy to open the front door and bring in the milk. He was too afraid, but she persisted. "Go ahead," she said. "God is outside and He will protect you." The boy thought about that for a moment, and then moved his tiny hand toward the door. He fearfully turned the knob to open the door, reached his little hand into that cold, dark morning, and shouted, "If you're out there, God, hand me the milk!"

Courage ... One From the Heart

Preparing a child to courageously meet the challenges life will certainly offer is perhaps the single most important aspect of parenting. Courage is such an important quality in today's complex world of choices that it forms the very foundation upon which the child constructs her personality. In fact, both psychologist Alfred Adler and world leader Winston Churchill both said that it is the most important of all traits because it is the one on which all others depend. From the French word coeur, meaning "heart," courage is the "heart" that enables us to take risks. And it is through risk-taking that we are able to develop responsibility, cooperation, independence ... and whatever else we may strive for. In fact, we define courage in Active Parenting Now as:

The confidence to take a known risk for a known purpose.

Courage is a feeling. It is a feeling of confidence that motivates us to take risks, knowing that we have a chance to succeed, and that even if we fail, the risk was worth taking. Courage is not the absence of fear but the willingness to take a reasonable risk in spite of fear. Without this feeling of courage, we often find ourselves sitting on the sidelines, unwilling to take the risks inherent in any endeavor. Without courage, we let life pass us by while we wishfully wait for someone else to "hand us the milk."

Courage and Fear

Courage first met fear
When I was still a child;
Courage gazed with cool, clear eyes;
Fear was something wild.

Courage urged, "Let's go ahead."
Fear said, "Let's turn back."
Courage spoke of what we had;
Fear of what we lacked.

Courage took me by the hand
And warmed my frozen bone;
Yet Fear the while tugged at my legs
And whispered, "We're alone."

Many have been the obstacles
Since first I had to choose,
And sometimes when Courage led me on
I've come up with a bruise.

And many have been the challenges
Since Fear and Courage met,
And yet those times I've followed Fear,
Too often—tagged along Regret.

Michael H. Popkin

Self-Esteem ... One From the Mind

Where does courage come from? It comes from a belief in ourselves that we are lovable, capable human beings who will eventually succeed. And even if we fail, we are still lovable, capable human beings. This belief in ourselves is commonly called "self-esteem." In other words we hold ourselves in high regard. When we think well of ourselves, when we think we have a good chance to succeed, then it makes sense that we will have the courage to take risks.

High Self-Esteem  **COURAGE**

This courage usually produces more positive behaviors, including the perseverance to keep trying when the going gets tough. The result is often success and positive feedback from others, which strengthens self-esteem and courage in a success cycle.

SUCCESS CYCLE

As we can see in the graphic, a success cycle doesn't mean that our children will never run into problems or failure, but rather, that they will be able to handle these problems effectively and eventually succeed. The opposite of a success cycle might be called a failure cycle. When self-esteem is low, kids often lack the courage to take positive risks and either fail to try at all, or turn to easier misbehavior to reach their goals. Such behavior often produces failure and negative feedback from others, which lowers self-esteem further and produces more discouragement in a downward spiral of failure.

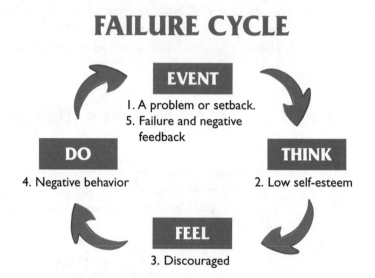

FAILURE CYCLE

EVENT
1. A problem or setback.
5. Failure and negative feedback

THINK
2. Low self-esteem

FEEL
3. Discouraged

DO
4. Negative behavior

Two Kinds of Character

Where does the concept of character fit into all of this? First, it is helpful to recognize that when we speak of character, we are really talking about two different things. The first definition might be something like this:

Character is the sum total of a person's
values, beliefs, attitudes, actions, and personality traits.

This is what we mean when we speak of a person's "character." Is he courageous or cowardly? Can you count on her or not? Does he possess such qualities as honesty, responsibility, perseverance, cooperativeness, and respect? When we hear the term "character education" it usually refers to efforts to instill these and other qualities of positive character in children. We have been learning methods of instilling such qualities throughout this program, because these qualities enable our children to survive and thrive in our modern society. Positive qualities of character run throughout the think-feel-do cycle and help to propel children (and adults) into success cycles.

This is usually good for the child, the family, and the community. However, it is also possible in our society to have high self-esteem, courage, and many other positive character traits, and yet still choose to break the rules, live outside the law, and otherwise reject the limits of society. This is why we also want our children to develop a second definition of character:

Character is the courage to do the right thing
even when you could get away with doing the wrong thing.

If we have not instilled in our children the values and beliefs of good character, then no amount of discipline or rewards is going to be sufficient.

Many people in our society only obey the law because they fear punishment if they break the law and get caught. This is not character; it's fear. These same people would break the law if they thought they could get away with it. In fact many rules, laws, and norms of morality are broken every day by people who think they can get away with it, and often do. In fact, most of us fall short at times of this definition of character. However, it is a worthy goal to work toward, and one worth instilling in our children. After all, we aren't always there looking over their shoulders. If we have not instilled in them the values and beliefs of good character—the integrity to do the right thing just because they believe it is the right thing to do—then no amount of discipline or rewards is going to be sufficient. Eventually they will succumb to the temptation and pressure to become harmfully involved with tobacco, alcohol and other drugs, reckless sexuality, violence, and other dangerous and hurtful behaviors.

Remember the list of 40 Developmental Assets we introduced in Chapter One? This list, developed by The Search Institute, presents assets that are key to preventing negative outcomes in child and youth development. These internal assets include commitments, values, competencies, and self-perceptions that, if nurtured within young people, provide them with "internal compasses" to guide their behaviors and choices.

Search Institute's 40 Developmental Assets for Children

SUPPORT

1. **Family Support**
Family life provides high levels of support

2. **Positive Family Communication**
Young person and her or his parent(s) communicate

3. **Other Adult Relationships**
Children have support from at least one adult other than their parents, and parents have support from people outside the home.

4. **Caring Neighborhood**
Children experience caring neighbors.

5. **Caring Out-Of-Home Climate**
School and other activities provide caring, encouraging environments for children.

6. **Parent Involvement in Out-of-Home Situations**
Parents are actively involved in helping children succeed in school and in other situations outside the home.

EMPOWERMENT

7. **Community Values Children**
Children feel that the family and community value and appreciate children.

8. **Children are Given Useful Roles**
Children are included in age-appropriate family tasks and decisions and are given useful roles at home and in the community.

9. **Service to Others**
Children serve others in the community with their family or in other settings.

10. **Safety**
Children are safe at home, at school, and in the neighborhood.

BOUNDARIES and EXPECTATIONS

11. **Family Boundaries**
The family has clear rules and consequences and monitors children's activities and whereabouts.

12. **Out-of-Home Boundaries**
Schools and other out-of-home environments provide clear rules and consequences.

13. **Neighborhood Boundaries**
Neighbors take responsibility for monitoring children's behavior.

14. **Adult Role Models**
Parents and other adults model positive, responsible behavior.

15. **Positive Peer Observation**
Children interact with other children who model responsible behavior and have opportunities to plan and interact in safe, well-supervised settings.

16. **Appropriate Expectations for Growth**
Adults have realistic expectations for children's development at this age.

CONSTRUCTIVE USE of TIME

17. **Creative Activities**
Parents, caregivers, and other adults encourage children to achieve and develop their unique talents.

18. **Out-of-Home Activities**
Children spend one hour or more each week in extracurricular school activities or structured community programs.

19. **Religious Community**
The family attends religious programs or services for at least one hour per week.

20. **Positive, Supervised Time at Home**
Children spend most evenings and weekends at home with their parents in predictable, enjoyable routines.

Search Institute's 40 Developmental Assets for Children (cont'd)

COMMITMENT to LEARNING

21. Achievement Expectation and Motivation
Children are motivated to do well in school and other activities.

22. Children are Engaged in Learning
Children are responsive, attentive, and actively engaged in learning.

23. Stimulating Activity
Parents and teachers encourage children to explore and engage in stimulating activities. Children do homework when it's assigned.

24. Enjoyment of Learning and Bonding with School
Children enjoy learning and care about their school

25. Reading for Pleasure
Children and an adult read together for at least 30 minutes a day. Children also enjoy reading or looking at books or magazines on their own.

POSITIVE VALUES

26. Caring
Children are encouraged to help other people.

27. Equality and Social Justice
Children begin to show interest in making the community a better place.

28. Integrity
Children begin to act on their convictions and stand up for their beliefs.

29. Honesty
Children begin to value honesty and act accordingly.

30. Responsibility
Children begin to accept and take personal responsibility for age-appropriate tasks

31. Healthy Lifestyle and Sexual Attitudes
Children begin to value good health habits and learn healthy sexual attitudes and beliefs as well as respect for others.

SOCIAL COMPETENCIES

32. Planning and Decision Making Practice
Children begin to learn how to plan ahead and make choices at appropriate developmental levels.

33. Interpersonal Skills
Children interact with adults and children and can make friends. Children express and articulate feelings in appropriate ways and empathize with others.

34. Cultural Competence
Children know about and are comfortable with people of different cultural, racial, and/or ethnic backgrounds.

35. Resistence Skills
Children start developing the ability to resist negative peer pressure and dangerous situations.

36. Peaceful Conflict Resolution
Children try to resolve conflicts nonviolently.

POSITIVE IDENTITY

37. Personal Power
Children begin to feel they have control over things that happen to them. They begin to manage frustrations and challenges in ways that have positive results for themselves and others.

38. Self-Esteem
Children report having high self-esteem.

39. Sense of Purpose
Children report that their lives have purpose and actively engage their skills.

40. Positive View of Personal Future
Children are hopeful and positive about their personal future.

What Can Parents Do?

Helping our children get into success cycles and stay there is a goal for all parents. Helping our children develop the character to be successful within the rules and limits of society is a responsibility of all parents. It is therefore important for us to become skilled at encouraging the development of self-esteem, courage, and character. But what does that word "encouraging" really mean?

"En-courage" means to "instill courage." Rudolf Dreikurs once said "children need encouragement like plants need water."

Breaking the word into two parts, "en-courage" means to "instill courage." Rudolf Dreikurs once said "children need encouragement like plants need water." Encouragement is the fertilizer that nourishes our children's courage, self-esteem, character, and skills. Wherever it is applied, we see more growth in that area. Do you want your child to be a good reader? Encourage her reading. Do you want him to be honest? Encourage acts of honesty. What about responsibility, cooperation, and courage? Again, where you sprinkle encouragement you spur growth. The remainder of this chapter will help you strengthen your skills in this critical area of parenting.

Encouragement: "Catch 'em Doing Good"

Imagine yourself in this situation:

You are driving home in your car. Suddenly, in your rearview mirror you see a police car with blue lights flashing, and it is following you. Anxiously, you pull over, wondering what you did wrong. You notice your rapid heartbeat, the perspiration forming on your palms, your dry mouth. The policeman approaches your car window and asks for your driver's license. He looks at the license, then at you, and says, "You know, I've been on the force for 12 years, and it's always a pleasure to see a courteous driver. I pulled you over so I could congratulate you on the fine driving skill you showed back there in that traffic tangle at the freeway overpass. If every driver were as courteous and considerate as you, we could avoid lots of snarls and headaches. So I just wanted to say, 'Thanks.'"

What do you think your reactions would be to the policeman's comment?

    a. You would feel good about yourself; you'd be a little proud.

    b. You would feel that you are a pretty good driver.

    c. You would feel encouraged to drive more courteously and considerately in the future.

    d. You'd almost faint from the shock!

Because most of us are not natural-born encouragers, we need to work at recognizing our own discouraging tendencies while strengthening our ability to encourage.

The chances are response "d" was your strongest. We just do not expect to receive such compliments from authority figures. And yet, in the above example, after the shock has worn off and you are driving away, you probably would feel good about yourself, think that you are a pretty good driver, and feel encouraged to drive more courteously and considerately in the future.

The policeman's comment was an example of the power of encouragement. With only a few words, he increased your self-esteem, gave a boost to your confidence, and created the likelihood that you would drive even better in the future. No wonder some call encouragement "the subtle giant."

The down side of encouragement is that in every opportunity to encourage our children (as well as ourselves and others) there is also an opportunity to discourage them or "remove courage." Because most of us are not natural-born encouragers, we need to work at recognizing our own discouraging tendencies while strengthening our ability to encourage. Before we look further at encouragement, let's consider its opposite—discouragement—and the ways it affects children's behavior.

Avoid Discouraging

The misbehaving child is usually a discouraged child.

The misbehaving child is usually a discouraged child. Somewhere along the line, he has lost the courage to face life's problems with positive behavior. As we saw in Chapter Four, such children have come to believe that the only path open to them is the easier, negative approach to their goals. They use undue attention-seeking, rebellion, revenge, and avoidance behaviors because they fear they will fail if they attempt the more difficult positive approaches.

In order to build children's self-esteem, courage, and character, we want to first become aware of some common ways we may be discouraging them.

In order to build children's self-esteem, courage, and character, we want to first become aware of some common ways we may be discouraging them. Referring again to the think-feel-do cycle, if we become discouraging events in our children's lives, we tend to lower their self-esteem, which leads to discouragement, which leads to negative behavior ... which may prompt us to become even more punishing and discouraging. To change this cycle, we want to do our best to become encouraging events in our children's think-feel-do cycle. Although abuse and neglect are the most serious form of discouragement, we are going to focus our attention on four less obvious ways that parents discourage their children and these can be turned into methods of encouragement.

DISCOURAGING EVENTS	ENCOURAGING EVENTS
Overprotection and pampering	**Stimulating Independence**
Focusing on mistakes	**Building on strengths**
Expecting too little	**Showing Confidence**
Expecting too much (perfectionism)	**Valuing the child as is**

If somebody who is important to you spends too much time telling you how dangerous and difficult the world is, you may come to believe that you can't handle things for yourself. You may let him handle problems for you, depriving you of a chance to learn from the experience. If you get in trouble at school or with the law, he is there to bail you out. And if you never experience the consequences of your mistakes, you begin to get the idea that you can do anything you like. But strangely you find yourself not feeling very confident, though you may act over-confident to make up for it.

If you find that your parents are constantly waiting on you, picking up after you, reminding you of things and otherwise pampering you, you come to expect that treatment from others. When they do not treat you the same, you find that things start falling through the cracks and mistakes multiply. You become angry and blame others, then wonder why your relationships are not satisfying. Statements like the following may be well intentioned, but they are counterproductive:

> *"Sure, I'll be glad to go down to the school and talk to your teacher. I'm sure when she realizes how hard you worked, she'll change your grade."*
>
> *"I shouldn't have to call you three times to get up in the morning, but at least you're getting to school on time."*

How to stimulate independence

Haim Ginott wrote, "Dependence breeds hostility."

Independence, or the ability to stand on one's own two feet, is essential for thriving in our modern society. In fact, when we keep our children overly dependent on us, not only do they pay a price, but so do we. As psychologist Haim Ginott wrote, "Dependence breeds hostility." Overprotecting and pampering do not lead to the appreciation that many parents expect. It leads to resentment! The last thing we want to do as parents is to keep our children overly dependent on us. Our job as parents is to work ourselves out of a job.

Our job as parents is to work ourselves out of a job.

As we encourage our children toward independence, we also want to keep in mind that they will benefit enormously by learning to cooperate, as we mentioned in Chapter One. The phrase, "no man is an island," expresses the truth that interdependence—independent individuals choosing to work together cooperatively—offers the best chance for success of both the individual and the human community.

Avoid pampering your child. When parents put themselves into the child's service or otherwise treat the child like a privileged character, the child eventually becomes dependent, spoiled, and discouraged. Some signs of

pampering a child include: calling her more than once to get up in the morning; routinely driving her places on short notice; picking out her clothes; giving her money on demand instead of an allowance; allowing her to curse at you or otherwise speak disrespectfully; not monitoring media such as TV, music, movies, and the internet; making her homework your responsibility; allowing her to frequently eat meals in front of the TV; always cleaning up after her; not requiring her to help with family chores; and rescuing her from the consequences of her misbehavior.

If you find some of these examples hitting home, then you can let your child know that you have decided to stop pampering her, and begin treating her more respectfully. You can do this in a firm yet friendly way, taking responsibility yourself, while even encouraging the child. For example:

Let your child know that you have decided to stop pampering her, and begin treating her more respectfully.

"I want to apologize for treating you like you didn't have the good sense to handle _____ (e.g., getting yourself up in the morning; your own money; your own homework; picking up your own clothes). From now on I'm going to stop treating you like a baby and leave it up to you."

"I don't use that kind of language when I'm angry with you; I don't expect you to use it when you are angry with me."

"I'll be glad to show you where dirty clothes go, but from now on I'm only washing the clothes that get put there."

Help the child develop a sense of interdependence. Life in our diverse, modern society is neither independent nor dependent. It is interdependent. We are all traveling in the same boat, and learning to work cooperatively with others is a key to individual success as well as the common welfare. You can invite cooperative behavior on the part of your child, with the aim of letting him experience the pleasure and benefits of group efforts.

"You're an important part of this family, and we'd like your ideas at family meetings."

"Why don't you come up on the sofa and snuggle with us?"

"Would you like to make lasagna with us?"

Allow natural consequences to teach. Children learn an amazing amount of valuable life lessons from direct experience of the consequences afforded by Mother Nature. This method of learning is so effective that it deserves a name: natural consequences.

> *Natural consequences are the results that naturally occur as a result of a child's behavior without the parent doing anything.*

Here are some examples:

> *The natural consequence of not eating breakfast is getting hungry before lunch.*
>
> *The natural consequence of oversleeping on a school day is being late for school.*
>
> *The natural consequence of leaving your bicycle outside may be that it gets rusty or that it is stolen.*

Natural consequences are particularly effective for teaching independence because the parent can be a sympathetic third party, rather than the disciplinarian. Of course, to be effective we have to avoid two temptations: 1) to rescue (for example, buy him a new bike); and 2) to say "I told you so." (How much better to say, "Gee, I know that's frustrating," rather than "I told you this would happen if you didn't put that bike away!")

When Natural Consequences Cannot Be Used as Teachers

There are many situations when our best course of action is to stay out of the way and let the natural consequences teach the lesson. However, there are three circumstances in which a responsible parent cannot simply allow Mother Nature to take her toll:

There are many situations when our best course of action is to stay out of the way and let the natural consequences teach the lesson.

1. **When the natural consequences may be catastrophic.** For example, the natural consequences of running into a busy street may be death.

2. **When the natural consequences are so far into the future that the child is not concerned about the connection.** For example, the natural consequences of not brushing her teeth may lead to eventual tooth decay.

3. **When the natural consequences of a child's behavior affect others rather than the child.** For example, the child borrows your scissors and loses them.

In these situations the parent owns the problem, and it is up to the parent to use the discipline skills covered in Chapters Three and Four to take action to prevent such natural consequences from occurring or reoccurring.

Building on Strengths vs. Focusing on Mistakes

If somebody who is important to you spends a lot of time telling you what you do wrong, you come to believe there is more wrong with you than right. If that important person yells or sounds disgusted with you, it hurts even more. If he calls you names or attacks your character, you may begin to believe that you are as bad as he says that you are. Ironically, it becomes harder to do things right because you are so worried about making mistakes and creating further disappointment.

Maybe you have worked hard to correct a problem or improve your behavior and all she notices is what is still not right. You feel that your effort has not been appreciated, and wonder why you should bother to try again in the future. You lose motivation and your performance drops further, which prompts more discouraging comments until finally you feel like a certified loser.

> *"I notice you left your glass in the den again last night. How many times do I have to ask you to be more considerate?"*
>
> *"This doesn't look good where you colored outside the lines, does it?"*
>
> *"Did you notice how your man beat you down court for that easy basket? You've really got to hustle back on defense."*

Building on Strengths: The BANK Method

If you and your child are locked in a power struggle or revenge cycle and want to break out, find something about the child that you like.

Kids do need to know what mistakes they have made in order to learn from the experience and do better in the future. We are not suggesting that you never mention a mistake or misbehavior. The mistake most parents make is to point out the mistakes and misbehavior, but then ignore the successes and positive behavior. The key to building successful behavior, however, is to focus the majority of your feedback on what your kids are doing right. This builds their confidence and motivates them to want to keep improving. In fact, if you and your child are locked in a power struggle or revenge cycle and want to break out, find something about the child that you like. Focusing your attention on what's right with your children, rather than what is wrong, is tremendously encouraging. And, as we've seen, encouragement leads to improved self-esteem, which leads to courage and positive behavior ... in other words, a success cycle.

The BANK Method of Encouragement

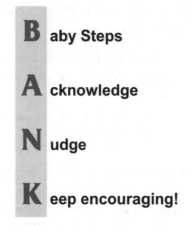

B aby Steps

A cknowledge

N udge

K eep encouraging!

To help you remember how to use this important aspect of encouragement effectively keep in mind these four letters: B-A-N-K. Just as a bank is a place where resources are invested for growth, you can use the BANK method to help your child build her personal assets and grow into a successful human being. Let's look at the four letters one by one:

B for Baby steps. The key to building on strengths is to break the learning down into baby steps. Remember, you didn't learn to walk all at once. You learned step by step. This learning process is the same for most things. Whether it is helping a child learn to complete his homework, or teaching him to be honest, we can systematically build on strengths to help our children build skills, values, and character.

> *"I know school can be difficult, but if we break each assignment down into small steps you'll find that you can do it."*

> *"If we want to teach Dani to be honest, I think we need to take it day by day and encourage her every time she tells the truth when she could have lied or deceived us."*

It is much more effective to "catch 'em doing good" than our traditional approach of catching them doing bad.

A for Acknowledge what your child does well. Once you have identified a goal for your child (for example, having good study habits or being an honest individual), get an idea where the child is on the path towards reaching that goal. It is unlikely that he can't read a single word or answers every question with a lie—so he will be somewhere in between. Now you have a place to start. Acknowledge what he can already do well in order to build confidence and motivation to take the next step.

> *"This is terrific! You've completed two assignments. This is the way to get ahead at school. I can really see that you've worked hard at this, but then I know you can work hard . . . I've seen you on the basketball court."*

> *"I'm not thrilled that you borrowed my hammer without asking, but I do appreciate your owning up to it when I asked. I appreciate your honesty."*

It is much more effective to "catch 'em doing good" than our traditional approach of catching them doing bad. In addition to acknowledging their progress, it also helps to acknowledge other areas where the child is already experiencing some success. This helps build the self-esteem that translates into risk taking and other successes. The parent who brought in the basketball connection in the previous example was using this strength-building technique effectively.

Examples like the following offer children a healthy diet of encouragement:

"It was really a pleasure having you out to dinner with us tonight. Your manners were great. Let's do it again soon."

"Thank you for helping with the dishes."

"I appreciate your playing quietly while I took a nap. That was very considerate."

"It sure is fun to play with you when you take turns with me."

N for Nudge the child to take the next step. Children get a sense of self-esteem from learning, whether they are learning a sport, a school subject, or a skill. As we have seen, learning requires many steps and gradual improvement. It also requires risk, because with each new step, there is the potential for failure. Even with children who have strong self-esteem, there are times when fear of failure paralyzes them, making it difficult to take the next step. And there are times for all of us when the frustration of not progressing the way we'd like undermines our courage to persevere and tempts us to give up. This is when an encouraging nudge from a parent or teacher can help give the child enough courage to take the next baby step. For example:

"Learning to do division can be frustrating, and I guess you feel like giving up. But if you'll just stick with it, I know you'll get it. Look how far you've come already! Now, how about tackling that last problem again?"

"I know it hasn't been easy, but you've really improved in being honest with us. And we're feeling like we can trust you more. So, if you still want to spend the night at Carrie's house, it's okay with us."

"You can do it. Go ahead."

"Keep trying. You'll get it."

"Let's take a break then try again."

"Sometimes a rest can help. Let's try again tomorrow."

K for Keep encouraging improvement and effort. Arthur Blank, co-founder of the tremendously successful Home Depot and owner of the Atlanta Falcons pro football team once said that although he is a highly competitive person, he never sees the finish line. In other words, life is a process where success is measured in growth and improvement rather than any single end result. The mistake most people make in the encouragement process is to wait until the child attains a desired goal before offering encouragement. One misguided father actually said that he was waiting for his son to graduate before complimenting him on his school work!

Any improvement, no matter how small, is a step in the right direction and should be noticed and acknowledged.

Since a key to encouragement is to break the process down into baby steps, it is important to offer encouragement along the entire route. Any improvement, no matter how small, is a step in the right direction and should be noticed and acknowledged. Since success is a great motivator, we want the child to be able to experience numerous successes along the way. This builds self-esteem and keeps the child moving towards the goal. If the child falls back a step (and that's to be expected) she needs our encouragement to keep at it and not give up. In fact, her effort alone, even when she's not making progress, should always be encouraged.

> *"Great! You are really getting good at writing down all of your assignments. One more day and you'll have a whole week."*

> *"Thanks for telling us about not turning in your homework on Monday. That took a lot of courage. We'll talk about what to do about it in a minute, but first I want you to know how much we admire your efforts to be more honest."*

> *"I can really see the effort that went into this."*

> *"Hey, this room is really looking good. You've gotten all your books picked up, and the bed's made. If you like, I have some time and could help you figure out a system for organizing your closet."*

> *"I really like the way you stick with it."*

Showing Confidence vs. Expecting too Little

If people who are important to you don't believe in your ability, you probably won't believe in it either. They don't have to say so; you can usually tell what they think of you by the way they act around you and the words they use with you. You pick up on those things pretty easily. If they never ask your opinion you guess that they don't think you have much useful to say. If they seem satisfied with half-hearted efforts at school, you figure they think that mediocrity is all you are capable of. If they do not encourage you to participate in a sport or other activity, you can sense that they don't think you can handle it. Of course, sometimes they make their opinions of you crystal clear by saying such things as:

> *"No, you can't use that! You'll break it."*
>
> *"I guess you're just not the type who does well in school."*

How To Show Confidence

When those we value most show confidence in our abilities we tend to gain confidence in ourselves.

A cornerstone of self-esteem and courage is the belief that we are capable of success, whether it is in school, at work, with friends, family, or a love relationship. As we achieve success in solving life's problems and learning new skills, our belief in ourselves grows. But tackling problems and attempting new skills takes confidence. When those we value most show confidence in our abilities we tend to gain confidence in ourselves.

There was a famous experiment in which teachers were told that results from an intelligence test showed that some of the students in their classes were highly intelligent and capable of excellent work while others were not. What the teachers did not know was that the results of the intelligence test had nothing to do with which students they were told were brighter. In fact, the students had been assigned at random. At the end of the year the students' grades were compared. Guess which group did better? As you might expect, the students in the so-called "intelligent" group had higher grades. The teacher's expectation that they were capable had made a significant difference in the students' ability to succeed. Such is the power of positive expectations on performance.

Parents can also help their children succeed by showing confidence in them. Here are some ways to do this:

Give responsibilities in line with what you know about your child's abilities.

Give responsibility. Giving your child responsibility is a nonverbal way of showing confidence. It is a way of saying, "I know you can do this." Of course, you want to give responsibilities in line with what you know about your child's abilities, or the standards may be set too high. Here are some examples of giving responsibility in ways that demonstrate confidence:

> *"I will agree to your keeping the dog, Julie, if you will accept the responsibility of feeding and caring for her."*
>
> *"I think you have handled getting yourself up in the morning really well, so you can probably handle staying up later now—say, 9:00 p.m. What do you think?"*

When you ask your child's opinion, you are demonstrating confidence in his ability to make a useful contribution.

Ask your child's opinion or advice. Children like to have parents lean on their knowledge or judgment. When you ask your child's opinion, you are demonstrating confidence in his ability to make a useful contribution. If you ask your child to teach you something, it shows confidence in his knowledge and skills. Asking for his opinions in such ways helps bolster his self-esteem:

> *"Which route do you think would be best on our trip to visit Grandma and Grandpa?"*
>
> *"What would you like to do with the toys that get left on the floor?"*
>
> *"Would you teach me how to play the new video game?"*
>
> *"Well, what were the reasons for the Civil War?"*

Avoid the temptation to take over. It is an act of confidence in our children's abilities when we refuse to step in and take over when they become discouraged. What a temptation it is, this tendency to relieve their discomfort by doing the thing that is so hard for them and so easy for us! But when we give in to the temptation, we are not showing confidence in the child. If we do something for the child on a regular basis that she, with a little persistence, could do independently, then we are communicating a lack of confidence in her ability to follow a task through to the end. When we bail her out of the consequences of misbehavior, we rob her of an important lesson in responsibility. We say in effect that we don't have confidence in her ability to handle the consequences of her actions.

All in all, taking over is not a way to encourage children who are discouraged; it is a way to certify their discouragement. Such children often show an inability to tolerate frustration. When things don't work out immediately, they give up—often having a "frustration tantrum" in which they are overwhelmed with anger and frustration at their inability to accomplish a task. Instead, encourage your child to stick with it with words such as these:

> *"Keep trying, you can do it!"*
> *"No, I can't stop the kids from teasing you, but I can talk to you about some things that you can do."*

Expect success and positive behavior. Like the teachers in the study who expected certain students to succeed, your expectations of your children are powerful influencers of their behavior. In fact,

Children often live up or down to our expectations.

Your expectations of your children are powerful influencers of their behavior.

So, why not expect them to succeed? When you let them know that you think they can do it—whether "it" is doing well in school, being polite in social situations, following family rules and values, or anything else—you are encouraging them to live up to your expectations. They will sometimes mess up, and they will need your encouragement not to give up when this happens. And of course, you want to keep your expectations in line with reality. After all, expecting a child to go

from Cs and Ds to straight As overnight is setting you both up for failure. But expecting that your child can improve and using the BANK method to encourage his improvement is a recipe for success.

"I know you can improve your grades if you set your mind on it."

"I'm counting on you to use your best manners when we are at Grandma's."

"I expect you to tell me the truth."

"Just keep practicing and you'll get it."

Valuing the Child vs. Expecting Too Much (Perfectionism)

Positive expectations are important. However, if your parents expect more from you than you are able to give, you gradually stop trying because you know you will never be able to satisfy them. You may decide to make your

mark in other ways, like misbehaving. Since you can't be the best at being the best, maybe you will set your goal at being the best at being the worst. Or maybe you will decide to become a perfectionist yourself in a futile attempt to please your parents and yourself. Life becomes one big worry as you try harder and harder to succeed. But even when you do succeed, you cannot enjoy your success for fear of what challenge to your self-esteem is coming next.

"How did you misspell 'circus' when you got all the others right? If you'd really thought about it, you would have had a perfect paper."

"This isn't a bad report card. But with your potential, you could have done better."

"You've got to practice, practice, practice if you ever want to be a really good violinist."

How To Value the Child

A child's self-esteem does not spring from achievements alone. Much more important for most people is that they are accepted by significant people in their lives—that they belong. In fact, much of our effort to be successful is really fueled by our desire to win the acceptance of those significant people. Ironically, what most of us really want deep down inside is to be accepted for just being ourselves, not just for our achievements. This is what it means to feel a sense of belonging.

Children who feel accepted by their parents have a tremendous bedrock of self-esteem upon which to construct a healthy, happy life.

The baseball pitcher, Tim Wakefield, was once asked before pitching the biggest game of his young career if he was nervous. His answer was no, because, he reasoned, no matter what happened that night, the next day three things would still be true: his parents would still love him, his friends would still love him, and God would still love him. Armed with that core sense of self-esteem and acceptance for who he was, his success in life, as measured by personal satisfaction, was well on its way.

Children who feel accepted by their parents have a tremendous bedrock of self-esteem upon which to construct a healthy, happy life. Without it, some of the richest, most successful people in history have lived lives of quiet desperation, wondering why their successes were never satisfying.

The goal is to communicate to our children that win or lose, pass or fail, in the limelight or in the line-up, we are still their parents and we are glad of it. We all need this unconditional acceptance from someone, and if we don't get it from our parents, we need to get it someplace else: from a substitute parent, or even a therapist. For some, a belief in God fulfills this same human need for unconditional acceptance.

Separate worth from accomplishments. A child's worth is less a matter of what he does, and more a matter of who he is. You can let your child know that while you admire his successes and share disappointment in his failures, you love him for himself. You can put emphasis on the importance of participation in the activities themselves and not just on the results. You can encourage your child while he is doing a task instead of waiting until the task is completed.

> *"I'm glad you enjoy learning."*
> *"Playing your hardest is more important than winning."*
> *"Losing doesn't make a person a loser."*

There are no bad children, only bad behavior. Help them accept mistakes with a smile rather than a kick.

There are no bad children, only bad behavior.

Separate worth from misbehavior. Just as a child's worth is something different from the sum total of her accomplishments, it is also different from her misbehaviors. A useful way to approach this is with the attitude that there are no bad children, only bad behavior. If a child is labeled "bad" or "no good" he may eventually come to believe that the label is true. When this happens, bad behavior then becomes appropriate. After all, what should we expect from "bad" people but "bad" behavior? This self-fulfilling prophecy makes it vitally important that we refrain from labeling or shaming children for their mistakes or misbehavior. Children who grow up ashamed of themselves have a difficult time regaining their lost self-esteem and courage.

Mistakes, like misbehavior, are not indications of a lack of worth, but are actually part of growth and development. A mistake can teach a valuable lesson, showing a child what not to do in the future. We want to help children, especially perfectionists, learn to make friends with their mistakes. Mistakes, as we have said, are tools for learning, not crimes to be ashamed of.

Children (and adults) who are afraid of being imperfect actually retard their own growth and development. A perfectionist, according to one joke, is a person who won't attempt a foreign language until he can speak it fluently. As this quip implies, a fear of mistakes yields a fear of trying, which in turn

Help them accept mistakes with a smile rather than a kick.

yields less learning. Since one of our goals is to help children learn, we want to help them accept mistakes with a smile rather than a kick.

> *"No, you're not bad, but coloring on the walls is a bad thing to do. Let's find a good place to color."*
>
> *"When we get angry at you, it doesn't mean we don't like you. It means we don't like something you've done."*
>
> *"Mistakes are for learning. When we make a mistake, we don't blame. We correct it."*
>
> *"I guess you made a mistake. Well, let's see what you can learn from it."*

Independence, or the ability to stand on one's own two feet, is essential for thriving in our democratic society.

You can say and do things that show your child you love her for her unique self, and for no other reason.

Appreciate the child's uniqueness. Although it is important to teach children that all people are equal, that doesn't mean all people are the same. It is encouraging for your child to know that she is unique, special, one of a kind. You can appreciate your child's uniqueness by taking an interest in her activities. Most of all, you can say and do things that show your child you love her for her unique self, and for no other reason.

> *"Anyway, that's my opinion. What's yours?"*
>
> *"When I see you from a distance, I can tell it's you from your walk."*
>
> *"This room is really you! I could never have decorated it for you."*
>
> *"You are the only you in the whole world. What luck that you happen to be my daughter!"*
>
> *"I love you."*

Family Enrichment Activity: Letter of Encouragement

As a young Sunday School teacher, I became annoyed with the idea of having to give grades to my students. Grades seemed an inadequate way to express either their progress or the way I felt about them after sharing nine months together. I decided to write each of my students a personal letter to go with the grades. While writing the letters, I found myself describing the positive aspects of each child and how he or she was progressing. These "letters of encouragement" were received appreciatively as the children left for summer vacation.

I didn't think much more about the letters until four years later. I was at a reception when a woman approached me and introduced herself as the mother of one of my students from that same Sunday School class. "That letter you wrote Alice meant so much to her," she said. "You know she still has it on her bulletin board."

All of the encouragement skills discussed in this session could be considered as family enrichment activities. But somehow "putting it in writing" carries that extra weight that makes it special. In addition, the child can refer back to a letter of encouragement in the future and rekindle the warm feeling it generated, just as Alice did. This week's activity is to write a letter of encouragement to each of your children. Let your letter have the following characteristics:

- Write about your child's improvement in some area, not necessarily perfection.

- Write only truthful statements; don't say that the child has improved when he really hasn't.

- Be specific about what the improvements are.

- Write how the child's behavior has been helpful to others.

A sample letter might look like this:

Dear Ben,

Your mother and I have been noticing how well you are doing with your reading. We can really hear the improvement. All your hard work is really paying off! Pretty soon you will be able to read anything you want to all by yourself. You can't imagine how wonderful a thing that is, and we are so happy for you.

I am also proud of the way you are accepting responsibility for your schoolwork. You are taking time to do your homework every school night like we talked about. You are also giving it your best and not rushing to get it done. Your teacher seems to have noticed the improvement, also. That must make you feel good.

Thanks also for helping me clean up the garage the other day. You have grown to where you are a big help in getting things done. Plus, you have always been great company with your sense of humor and positive attitude. And if I forget to say it often enough, I'm real glad that you are my son.

Love,
Dad

Family Meeting: Character Talks

Building positive values and character in our children is a matter of using many of the skills in this book—from disciplining behavior that reflects negative values to encouraging behavior that reflects positive ones. We can do this in little ways throughout our everyday interactions with our children and through the examples we set through our own words and actions. But the notion that "values are caught, not taught" is only half true. Group discussion is a very effective way to teach values when done effectively.

Group discussion is a very effective way to teach values when done effectively.

This chapter's family meeting is to discuss an area of character as a family. These character talks, as we call them, are opportunities to understand and influence your child's developing beliefs and values that underlie the development of character. Topics can include anything that you think is important. For example: honesty, hard work, perseverance, courage, cooperation, patriotism, respect, health—all these things make up character which means doing the right thing when you could get away with doing the wrong thing.

To help you choose a topic for your character talk, refer to the list of character words on page 169. The following tips will help you get your first talk off to a good start.

1. Plan how you will introduce the topic, and write down points you want to cover. Starting a group discussion is often the most difficult part. It is helpful to plan how you will introduce the subject. Topics for future talks might be chosen by different family members, and each might prepare his own introduction. Be sure to list important points you want to make during the meeting so you don't forget them. A simple introduction for your first talk might go something like this:

We called this meeting because we want to take time now and then to talk about topics that are important to all of us—topics that have to do with the kind of people we are becoming. And I say "we" because parents are still growing and changing too. The topic I've chosen for our first talk is "courage."

2. Ask open-ended questions to stimulate discussion. Once you have introduced the topic, having a few good questions to ask can help launch the discussion. Prepare these ahead of time and make sure that they are open-ended. This means that they cannot be answered with a simple "yes" or "no." For example,

Closed questions:

> *"Do you think courage is important"?*
> *"Is fear always bad?"*

Open-ended:

> *"What are some ways that courage is important?"*
> *"When can giving in to fear get you in trouble?"*
> *"When do you think fear might be a good thing?"*
> *"What does courage mean? Is it just physical courage or are there other types of courage?"*

Remember to use your active communication skills from Chapter Two and listen with empathy.

3. Listen with empathy as you discuss the topic together. Remember to use your active communication skills from Chapter Two and listen with empathy to your child's thoughts and feelings. This will help develop his own emotional intelligence and encourage him to continue talking. Avoid communication blocks as you keep an open, nonjudgmental attitude about histhoughts and feelings. This is particularly important (and difficult) when he says something that goes against your own value system. However, if you are quick to judge or criticize (even nonverbally with a negative facial expression) you run the risk of shutting him down and limiting your chance to influence him.

> *"That's an interesting point. I hadn't thought of courage being used like that."*
> *"You must have been frightened when that happened, and yet you didn't quit."*
> *"I'm not sure I agree with you about that, but it does give me another way to look at it."*

4. Share your own values persuasively. Children today are less likely to automatically accept our values and beliefs just because we tell them.

The more relevant you can make your examples to your child's experience, the better chance you have of getting through to her core beliefs and values.

Being a positive influence requires accurate information, sound reasoning, and persuasive arguments. Bringing in outside resources such as a relevant magazine article, a movie, or even a TV show can help lend weight to your point of view. Sometimes relating a personal experience can create a story in your child's mind that helps her learn an important lesson. The more relevant you can make your examples to your child's experience, the better chance you have of getting through to her core beliefs and values.

> *"I thought the character in that movie showed a lot of courage in standing up to his friends who wanted him to cheat on the exam."*

> *"When we don't try because we are afraid we'll fail, we don't even have a chance to succeed. Remember, you get some of what you go for, but you don't get any of what you don't go for."*

> *"To this day, I still have regrets about not trying out for the basketball team."*

5. **Find support materials.** Go to the library or surf the internet for information. Often, videos, audiotapes, booklets, and leaflets are available that can help you explain a subject to your child.

Family Activity: Making A Character Collage

One example of a fun family activity that can be used to end a family meeting is making a "character collage." This is a great way to reinforce the importance of qualities like courage, cooperation, honesty and respect while at the same time building on strengths and creating family cohesiveness. You'll need the following materials:

Magazines you don't mind cutting up

A pair of scissors for each person (or enough to share)

A piece of white poster board

Glue, paste, or rubber cement (enough to easily share)

Collages are made by cutting out words and pictures from the magazines to represent a character trait or traits that you have chosen as your theme. By pasting these words and pictures onto your poster board at various angles you can create an artistic work that is fun to make and keep. Personalize the piece by cutting out letters (or if you can find a complete word) to make the name of the person (or family) who the collage will belong to.

The following are a few of the types of collages that you might make:

Collages are made by cutting out words and pictures from the magazines to represent a character trait or traits that you have chosen as your theme.

A Family Collage. Use the entire poster board (approx. 17 x 22) to make a collage of a single character word, such as "courage," or as many that you can find that apply to your family. Make sure everyone in the family contributes by finding words and pictures in the magazines and helps with the gluing. To personalize the collage even further, add a photo of your family to the middle of the board with your family name spelled out in letters cut from the magazines.

Personal Collages. You can do the same activity with each family member making his own collage. Again, choose a trait or traits and look for words and pictures that represent the picture in some personal way. For example, if you play basketball and the word is "courage," you might find a picture of someone playing basketball to include on your collage, because it takes courage to learn a sport. Be sure to label the collage with the person's name, the character quality (or qualities), and if you choose, a picture of the person. You may also decide to use a half sheet of poster board for these collages since they are individual.

Personal Collages with a Twist. You can turn this activity into an encouragement exercise with a simple twist: no one is allowed to cut out words or pictures for his or her own collages. Each person can only find words or pictures for someone else in the family. For example, someone might find a picture of a mother at work and cut it out to give to the mother in the family with the words "hard working" cut out to go with it. When everyone has enough pictures and words, each person arranges their own collage and glues it down.

Feel free to be creative and come up with other types of collages. The key is to help family members visualize themselves and each other actively demonstrating qualities of positive character. Not only will your kids enjoy the activity, but once the collage is finished and hung on a wall, it will create a lasting impression of your family values.

Chapter 5

HOME ACTIVITIES

- Practice "stimulating independence" and complete the guide sheet on page 214.

- Practice "building on strengths" and complete the guide sheet on page 215.

- Practice "showing confidence" and complete the guide sheet on page 216. (optional)

- Find ways to show that you value your child as he or she is, and complete the guide sheet on page 217. (optional)

- Write each of your children a letter of encouragement and complete the guide sheet on page 219.

- Have a family meeting "character talk" about courage and complete the guide sheet on page 218.

- Remember to "take care of the caregiver" and add to the chart on page 195.

In the former USSR during its days under Communist dictatorship the people had few freedoms. In fact, they were not even free to leave the country and live elsewhere. A popular story circulated through Europe during this time about how a Soviet Premier was out fishing by himself one day in a small boat. Trying to pull in a large fish, he lost his balance and fell into the water. Unable to reach his boat, he would surely have drowned had it not been for the heroics of a young woman in a nearby boat of her own. After his rescue, the grateful Premier tells the woman who he is and offers to grant her anything in his power as a reward for saving his life. "In that case," says the courageous young woman, "I would like for you to open the borders for a single day and let anyone who wants to leave do so."

"Aha!" replies the smiling leader, "You want to be alone with me."

Today, the former Soviet Union is made up of free states that allow its citizens many rights, including the right to leave. In fact, the allure of freedom has been a powerful force throughout history as one people after another have chosen democracy for their government. Active Parenting Now has stressed the importance of preparing our children to live successfully within such societies, whether in the United States, Russia, Canada, Japan, Korea, Sweden, or anyplace else that embraces the principles of democracy. Because the purpose of Active Parenting Now is to support you in instilling qualities in your children that will enable them to survive and thrive in a democracy, what better place to begin teaching democratic principles than in the family?

But what are the principles of a democracy? See if you agree with our understanding of the democratic process:

Principles of Democracy

Principles of Democracy						
	In a Democratic Society			**In an Active Parenting Family**		
	Yes	No	Comments	Yes	No	Comments
Equality is a prized value.	✓		"All...are created equal." The Declaration of Independence by Thomas Jefferson.	✓		Remember..."equal" does not mean "the same."
Citizens are free to do whatever they please.		✓	There are limits to freedom and consequences for breaking the laws set by the leaders...even for the leaders (that's equality again).		✓	There is "freedom within expanding limits." Even parents must accept some limits and abide by consequences.
All citizens vote on everything.		✓	The elected leaders do most of the decision making.		✓	Parents are the leaders and they, too, must make most decisions.
All citizens have a voice and can influence the decisions of their leaders.	✓		Most elected leaders are highly sensitive to the opinions of their constituents.	✓		Active parents listen to the opinions of their children, and allow them to influence family decisions.
Everyone can vote for their leaders.		✓	Only adults vote. Only citizens vote.		✓	There are no voting booths in the womb. Children do not choose their parents.

Freedom of Speech

Democracy doesn't mean you will always get your way;
it means you will always get your say.

The feeling on the part of children that their voices and opinions make a difference builds cooperation and responsibility.

One of the themes stressed in *Active Parenting Now* is the importance of allowing children a voice in decisions that affect their lives. Just as freedom of speech is a basic freedom in our democratic society, a cooperative household must allow its members the same freedom. Of course, democracy doesn't mean you will always get your way; it means you will always get your say. By allowing children to influence our decisions through respectful discussion, we are better able to maintain our parental authority.

The feeling on the part of children that their voices and opinions make a difference builds cooperation and responsibility, and at the same time it makes anger and rebellion less likely. This chapter will present three types of family discussion that will offer you and your children opportunities for communicating as a cooperative unit:

The Importance of Family Meetings

With more and more children running away from home and so many marriages ending in divorce, it would be nice if there were one simple formula for keeping the family together. There isn't. But what might come closest is the following, although overstated, slogan:

When the family talks, nobody walks.

Talking together as a family is such an important part of thriving in a democratic society that we suggest you begin holding family meetings as soon as your children are old enough to participate (usually by about age seven).. These meetings can be grouped under five types:

Informal Meetings. These are informal, quick meetings to make a decision about something affecting the family in the near future. In Chapter One, we introduced this type of family meeting to decide on a Family Enrichment Activity, Taking Time for Fun. In Chapter Two, we talked about having a simple Family Meeting to set the Bedtime Routine together.

Problem-Prevention Discussions. We introduced this type of talk in Chapter 3 as a method of anticipating and preventing problems before they happen.

Problem-Solving Discussions. This type of discussion was introduced in Chapter 4 as a structured method of handling problems that do occur.

Character Talks. Presented in Chapter 5, these are discussions aimed at building positive character traits and values in your children.

Family Council Meetings. These are more formal meetings that will be covered later in this chapter

Whether you choose to begin with the less formal family meetings and problem-solving discussions, or to plunge right in with the family council meeting, it's important you make the effort to begin.

In this chapter, we'll also fill in a little more information about Family Meetings, and provide some helpful tips and suggestions for making these discussions successful in your family.

Four Good Reasons for Holding Family Meetings

When we first presented the Problem-Solving Model in Chapter Four, we saw that no matter whether the problem is owned by parent or child, it can still be handled in either a Problem-Solving Discussion or in a Family Council Meeting. By teaching our children to work cooperatively as a family in solving such problems we not only equip them to work better with others, but we actually find better solutions to family problems. It really is true that...

None of us are as smart as all of us.

1. **Cooperation.** Regular family meetings teach each person in the family that all are in the same boat, all on board can share in steering the boat, and the best way to decide how and where to steer it is to share feelings and opinions until an agreement is reached.

2. **Responsibility.** Regular participation in family meetings teaches each person in the family to make the best choices she can make on behalf of the family. After all, everyone will have to live with the consequences once the choices are made.

3. **Courage.** Family meetings are laboratories for individual courage. Each family member learns how important it is to say what he really thinks and feels, even if it isn't shared by anybody else. Meetings also provide opportunities for sharing encouragement.

4. **Self-esteem.** When children see their ideas valued and their participation welcomed, they think well of themselves. This self-esteem can carry over into other aspects of their lives.

How To Get Started With a Family Meeting

Whichever type of family meeting you are holding, parents are usually the ones to present the idea and get the meetings started. Here are some points for parents to consider in setting up a family meeting.

Start with those who are willing to attend. In some situations, a few family members are not ready to discuss matters in a family meeting, or they feel the idea is not a good one. But this doesn't mean the idea should be abandoned. Family meetings can still be held, if most family members agree on holding them. Those who do not attend the early meetings may decide to attend later when they see the advantages.

Who should attend family meetings? Family meetings should include parents, children, and anyone else who lives with the family, such as grandparents, uncles, or aunts. In other words, anyone who has a stake in decisions affecting the daily life of the family should be present.

Families affected by separation or divorce can still hold family meetings, even though one parent will not be participating.

Single–parent households. Families affected by separation or divorce can still hold family meetings, even though one parent will not be participating. In those cases it is important for the family to avoid discussing matters pertaining to the children's relationship with the absent parent. Those matters are owned by the children and the absent parent. Such problems should be handled by active communication, away from the family meeting.

Time and place. Select a time and a place convenient and agreeable to everyone who will be attending. A good time for family meetings is Sunday afternoons, the beginning of the week. The family is more likely to be together at that time, and the past week can be reviewed, the upcoming week anticipated. The meetings should be held in a place comfortable for all participants, preferably around a table with enough room to pull up a chair.

Communication Tips

DO:
- Speak respectfully
- Invite everyone's ideas
- Share how you think and feel
- Encourage others

DON'T:
- Put anyone's ideas down
- Interrupt
- Monopolize the discussion
- Consider only your point of view
- Criticize others
- Call anyone names

Helping our children learn to be effective problem solvers will give them a tremendous advantage in a democratic society.

Once you establish ground rules for your family talks, it will be easier to keep everyone in a positive framework. If a child violates one of these rules in a meeting, simply remind him with a firm, calm comment such as, "Didn't we agree that we wouldn't criticize each other?"

Leadership Roles

There are two leadership roles at family meetings:

1. **Chairperson.** Keeps the discussion on track and sees that everybody's opinion is heard.

2. **Secretary.** Takes notes during the meeting, writes the minutes after the meeting, and reads the minutes at the next meeting.

These two duties can be assumed by the parents at the first meeting. After that, other family members should take turns at being chairperson and secretary in an agreed-upon order, so that no one person is in charge every time.

How To Be an Effective Chairperson: A Guide for Family Members

Just follow the agenda:

1. **Compliments.** Ask if anyone appreciates something a family member said or did during the past week. This is a time for members of the family to say thanks to each other for good deeds and to encourage each other with compliments.

2. **Minutes.** Ask the person who was secretary last week to read the minutes aloud. The minutes remind everyone of what happened at the last meeting.

3. **Old business/new business.** Ask the family to talk about any matter that wasn't finished at the last meeting. These unfinished matters are called "old business." Let each person say what he or she wants to say, but remind people that they should not talk when someone else is talking.

Next, ask the family to talk about matters that have been written on the agenda. You should read pages 128 through 131 to learn a good method of solving any problems that may come up.

4. **Allowances.** This is a good time for Mom or Dad to pass out allowances.

5. **Treat or family activity.** End the meeting by saying, "The meeting is adjourned." People get tired if meetings go on too long, so keep your meeting to an agreed-upon time limit. We recommend 10-15 minutes with younger children (5- to 7-year-olds) and increasing to 30-45 minutes with older children. Usually, your family will want to play a game or have a dessert after the meeting so you can end on a positive note.

How To Be an Effective Secretary: A Guide for Family Members

To be an effective secretary, you need to do only three things:

1. **Listen carefully to what is said.**

2. **Write down what is decided on each matter that is discussed.**

3. **Later (after the meeting), write a summary of what was decided. This summary is called "the minutes." Read the minutes aloud at the next meeting.**

Here is what the minutes may look like:

<u>Minutes of Family Meeting, March 14th</u>

Chairperson was Jerry. Secretary was Linda. The family decided that:

1. We would go to Lake Lure this summer for vacation.

2. Jerry will pay Linda $5 for the lost book.

3. We will wait until the next meeting to decide whether we want to go on the weekend hike in April with the hiking club.

The Family Council Meeting

The Family Council Meeting is a time, once a week, when the entire family gathers to make plans and handle problems that affect family members.

The types of family meetings that we have previously discussed are useful methods of bringing your family together for specific, time-limited purposes. They may also be incorporated into the Family Council Meeting. The Family Council Meeting offers an ideal forum in which all family members participate in resolving problems and making family decisions.

Simply stated, the Family Council Meeting is a time, once a week, when the entire family gathers to make plans and handle problems that affect family members. It can last from 20 minutes to an hour and is conducted according to an agenda. In effect, it is what a business meeting is to an organization.

The first Family Council Meeting should be a short one. It's an excellent idea to have only one item of business at this meeting: Plan an outing or a time for fun together right after the meeting. Later meetings can be longer and follow a more extensive agenda.

Suggested Agenda

Here is an agenda that works for many families. We will elaborate on it more in the section "How To Be an Effective Chairperson." You can modify it to fit your circumstances.

1. **Compliments**

2. **Minutes**

3. **Old business/new business**

4. **Allowances**

5. **Treat or family activity**

New Business Agenda

A sheet of paper labeled "Agenda" can be taped to the refrigerator or posted at another convenient location.

A sheet of paper labeled "Agenda" can be taped to the refrigerator or posted at another convenient location.

Most families find that the new business section of the family meeting works better if items have been written on a posted agenda before the meeting. A sheet of paper labeled "Agenda" can be taped to the refrigerator or posted at another convenient location. When a problem occurs that a family member would like handled at the next family meeting, she writes it on the agenda. For example:

<u>New Business Agenda</u>

1. Why can't I spend the night with Melissa? -Sara

2. Sara keeps coming into my room without asking. -Jose

3. I need help with chores. -Mom

Agenda items are handled in order at the next family meeting. Items that are not brought up before the meeting is over can be carried over to the next meeting. Many times, an agenda item will have been handled by those involved before the meeting and can be dropped from the list.

One final benefit of having a written agenda is that it offers parents an excellent way of staying out of children's fights. When a child tries to engage you in solving one of his problems, you can sympathetically suggest that it be put on the agenda for this week's meeting.

> *Austin:* "Ben keeps taking my toys without asking. Tell him to stop."
>
> *Mother:* "Gee, honey, you sound pretty angry about that. Why don't you put it on the agenda for this week's family meeting?"

The ground rules for handling this type of problem during a family council meeting are exactly the same as during a problem-solving discussion. You can also use the same five steps for solving problems in a group that were presented on pages 128 through 131. When there are no pressing problems on the new business agenda, you may choose to use this time for a family talk.

Drugs, Sexuality, and Violence

The following is a true story that we retell in the Active Parenting of Teens version of this video-based program.

> There had been a lot of drinking at the party, including an open keg of beer that poured freely. Many of the teens were busily getting drunk in the front yard when a carload of uninvited guests arrived. These teens were from another high school and had also been drinking. They arrived angry that one of their girlfriends had come to the party with a date from the other school. Angry words quickly escalated into a fight with as many as 15-20 teenagers joining. Suddenly, one of the kids pulled out a knife and stabbed another boy in the stomach. Everything stopped as they rushed the victim to the hospital…where he died.

You may be thinking that too many parents leave their homes unattended, allowing teenagers to have unmonitored parties while they are out of town. While this is certainly true, it was not the case in this instance. The parents were home. Upstairs. Watching TV. When asked later why they had not been downstairs supervising their youngsters, they replied, "because we didn't want to get in the way."

Developing Protective Factors

In Active Parenting, we believe that it is the responsibility of parents to "get in the way."   As we said before, parents have four windows of opportunity in the Think-Feel-Do cycle to help us move children into success cycles. We'll talk more about parents "getting in the way" soon, but first let's look at another important way that parents can be positive influences in children's lives.

The Center for Substance Abuse and Preventon (CSAP) has identified numerous "protective factors" that exist in six different domains, or "life areas."   Research shows that the more of these protective factors that exist in a child's life, the less likely the child is to experiment with or become negatively involved with alcohol, tobacco, or other drugs (ATODs).

The chart on the next two pages details these protective factors by domain, and also presents ways that parents can help develop these factors in their children. The most obvious domain that parents can influence is the Family domain. However, as the chart shows, there are many ways that we can develop protective factors in the other domains as well. Please read over this chart carefully, and ask yourself the following questions:

How many of these actions am I already taking to develop these protective factors in my child?

How many of these actions could I start taking?

What skills do I need to learn or practice in order to be more effective in developing these factors in my child? (Chapter references are provided to review skills taught in this guide that will help you.)

Protective Factor	How parents can help develop them
INDIVIDUAL DOMAIN	
Positive personal characteristics, including: social skills and social responsiveness; cooperativeness; emotional stability, positive sense of self; flexibility; problem-solving skills; and low levels of defensiveness	• Work to instill qualities of good character in child (i.e. courage, character, self-esteem, and respect). *(Chapters 1 and 5)* • Encourage positive bonding with child. *(Family Enrichment Activities, All Chapters)* • Communicate expectations clearly, and listen actively. *(Active Communication; Chapter 2)* • Provide child with age-appropriate choices. *(Method of Choice: Chapter 1)* • Help child solve problems he owns, and involve child in solving family problems. *(Active Problem Solving, Chapter 4; Problem-Handling, Chapter 2)* • Build on child's strengths, and show confidence in child's ability. *(Chapter 5)* • Help child manage anger. *(Chapter 4)*
Bonding to societal institutions and values, including: attachment to parents and extended family; commitment to school; regular involvement with religious institutions; and belief in society's values	
Social and emotional competence, including: good communication skills, responsiveness; empathy; caring; sense of humor, inclination toward prosocial behavior; problem-solving skills; sense of autonomy; sense of purpose and of the future (e.g., goal-directedness); and self-discipline	
FAMILY DOMAIN	
Positive bonding among family members	• Express love and affection to child on a regular basis. Establish routines and be consistent with them. *(Bedtime Routines and "I Love You's," Chapter 2)* • Use positive discipline methods. *(Polite Requests, "I" Messages, Logical Consequences, and Firm Directions, Chapter 3)* • Emphasize family unit. *(Family Enrichment Activities, all Chapters)* • Involve child in family decisions and responsibilities. *(Family Meetings, All Chapters; Preventing Problems, Chapter 3)* • Encourage child in all areas, including school, and build on child's strengths. *(Chapter 5)* • Value child for who he or she is. *(Chapter 5)* • Communicate expectations clearly. *(Active Communication: Chapter 2)*
Parenting that includes: high levels of warmth and avoidance of severe criticism; sense of basic trust; high parental expectations; and clear and consistent expectations, including children's participation in family decisions and responsibilities.	
An emotionally supportive parental/family milieu, including: parental attention to children's interests; orderly and structured parent-child relationships; and parent involvement in homework and school-related activities	

PEER DOMAIN

Association with peers who are involved in school, recreation, service, religion, or other organized activities

- Encourage positive peer relationships.
- Expose child to opportunities to form positive peer relationships.
(Parents Filtering Negative and Influencing Positive Events, Chapter 6)

SCHOOL DOMAIN

Caring and support, sense of "community" in classroom and school

High expectations from school personnel

Clear standards and rules for appropriate behavior

Youth participation, involvement, and responsibility in school tasks and decisions

- Be involved in school activities.
- Be informed of what is happening in your child's school.
- Know your child's teachers, and attend parent-teacher conferences.
- Show your child that learning and school are a priority.
- Read with your child regularly.
- Encourage your child in schoolwork and learning. *(Chapter 5)*
- Build on child's strengths, and show confidence in child's ability. *(Chapter 5)*

COMMUNITY DOMAIN

Caring and support

High expectations of youth

Opportunities for youth participation in community activities

- Seek out and provide opportunities for child to participate in positive community activities
- Provide other adult mentors in your child's life
(Parents Filtering Negative and Influencing Positive Events, Chapter 6)

SOCIETY DOMAIN

Media literacy (resistance to pro-use messages)

Decreased accessibility

Increased pricing through taxation

Raised purchasing age and enforcement

Stricter driving-while-under-the-influence laws

- Monitor child's exposure to media. (TV, Internet, magazines, books, etc.)
- Provide child with positive media exposure and limit negative exposure.
- Discuss issues brought up in the media with child, especially regarding alcohol, tobacco, other drugs. Listen actively to his point of view, and share yours convincingly. *(Active Communication, Chapter 2)*
- Limit child's exposure to alcohol, tobacco, and other drugs (ATODs). *(Parents Filtering Negative and Influencing Positive Events, Chapter 6; Parents Affecting the Think-Feel-Do Cycle, Chapter 6)*

Based on the CSAP (Center for Substance Abuse and Prevention) model of Protective Factors for youth prevention. This information and related information are published at www.secapt.org

Getting in the Way: Parents Filtering Events

One purpose of this program is to instill qualities of character in our children that will enable them to make good decisions when events start getting out of hand. We have talked about handling problems in ways that move children into success cycles so that they can use their best thinking, feeling, and doing to meet such challenges. We have talked about the importance of not overprotecting kids, but allowing them to learn from the natural consequences of their actions as they develop into independent adults.

Active parents use their presence as filters to prevent dangerous events from influencing their children.

Even so, there are still times when parents should GET IN THE WAY! The technical term for this is interdiction, and it is no accident that it is often applied to the drug trade, as in "drug enforcement agents interdicted illegal drugs coming into the country." Just as governments try to filter out illegal drugs before they get into the system, active parents use their presence as filters to prevent dangerous events from influencing their children.

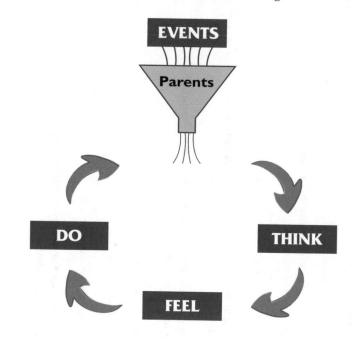

As the graphic shows, parents can sometimes come between events and their children, filtering their ability to influence the child's think-feel-do cycle. These include events that are excessively dangerous such as an unsupervised party with underage drinking for the teens in the earlier example. You are probably already tuned into many of these risks for younger children.

Examples of Excessively Dangerous Events

One type of excessively dangerous events includes physical risks such as:

- Climbing too high

- Swimming without supervision

- Riding without seatbelts or in unsafe vehicles

- Being left unsupervised in public places where they could be snatched or molested

- Being left around known bullies or other violent people

- Playing in a busy street or other unsafe place

- Being around poisons or other dangerous household objects

The second type of risk that we want to filter out as much as possible includes events that are likely to have a negative influence on the child's developing beliefs, attitude, values, and character. We want to be particularly vigilant to influences that might encourage the use of tobacco, alcohol or other drugs, reckless sexuality, and violence.

Examples of Negative Influences

Unrestricted use of media. This can include the internet, TV, movies, music, books, magazines, and games. The following tips can help:

- *Read rating systems and use them.* Don't cave in and allow kids to view more mature material than they are ready for. Make sure you have seen it first if you plan to make an exception to the rating guide.

Keep TVs and computers in public areas of the house so that you can easily check what is being viewed.

- *View, play, or listen to what your child is doing* from time to time to stay on top of what messages are being communicated. Then do not be afraid to limit those that are too sexual, violent, or otherwise run counter to your values. Discuss your reasons with your child and listen actively to theirs. But, as the parent, the final call is yours to make.

- *Keep TVs and computers in public areas of the house* so that you can easily check what is being viewed.

- *Watch some TV shows with your child* and use other media with them at times so that you can discuss important themes that come up.

- *Learn to use parental controls* provided by internet providers and other methods of monitoring what your child is watching.

- *Talk with the parents of your children's friends* and encourage them to be vigilant also. Kids will often seek out homes where the restrictions are lax, so support each other.

Peers and other "friends" who are known to break rules, encourage misbehavior, and even break laws. This is tricky because you do not want to try to dictate who your child's friends can be, which can easily lead to rebellion and sneaking. Avoid judging on the basis of looks alone.. However, let your child know that if she and another child get into trouble together, then they must not be having a good influence on each other. The logical consequence is to separate them for a time. Allow them to try again after a reasonable period if they still want to.

Adults whose values differ greatly from your own, even including adult friends, teachers, and clergy. While exposure to other people's ideas is healthy for children, you can reasonably attempt to limit your child from being around adults who display values that are grossly different from your own family values. Choose schools, religious institutions, and other places that support your values.

When you cannot limit these influences be sure to talk with your child about what he is exposed to in a way that presents your viewpoint. For example,

> *"I know Aunt Cathy smokes and she is a cool lady in a lot of ways, but smoking is a terrible thing for her to do to herself for all the reasons we have talked about."*

Getting In the Way: Parents Encouraging Events

No child gets everything he needs from his parents.

If parents can filter OUT certain negative events that might harm or negatively influence our children, we can also filter IN, or encourage, positive events that can help build character that leads to a success cycle. As much as we might like to think otherwise, no child gets everything he needs from his parents. Kids have to supplement what we give them with other adults and peers. Parents can help this process along by thinking of creative ways to provide encouraging influences on their children's development. For example:

Positive adult influences. Make sure that your child has positive contact with other adult mentors, such as:

- *Spiritual youth groups*
- *Sports coaches*
- *Teachers*
- *Adult friends*
- *Relatives, especially grandparents and others without young children of their own*
- *Mentoring programs such as Big Brother/Big Sister*

Media. There are many positive role models and lessons in books, movies, music, TV and the internet. Help your child find and take advantage of this positive input and you will strengthen many positive values.

Summer camp. Camp counselors and other staff can be a wonderful influence on children's development. Although, to be fair, I am particularly biased in favor of a camp experience having grown up as the son of a camp director. I always valued the lessons I learned from many of my own counselors, and have heard hundreds of adults, even one national leader, thank my father for the positive effect he had on their lives.

When delivered in a loving and supportive manner, a spiritual education will provide many positive lessons of character as well as faith.

A loving spiritual education. When delivered in a loving and supportive manner, a spiritual education will provide many positive lessons of character as well as faith.

A good academic environment. Let's face it—all schools are not created equal. Your children will spend more time at school than any other place other than their beds so find the best one that your financial situation will allow, even if it means moving. The value of a good educational environment is more than just the teachers and facilities. Just as important is the quality of the other kids and families that your child goes to school and plays with as they will also influence your child.

Family Enrichment Activity: Emphasizing the Family Unit

Active Parenting Now believes that families are the backbone of civilization and that your family is the most important family in the world …to your children. History has proven time after time that alone we could never survive, but by forming small cooperative units we could thrive. Families have been a source of belonging, learning, and contributing for children and for society—and, to a large extent, the measure of any civilization rests on the strength of its families.

So whether you are part of a traditional Mom-and-Dad family, or whether it's a blended stepfamily, a single-parent family, or any other style of family—it's important for you to look for ways to let your children know that they are part of a family unit. Plan frequent family activities; use phrases like "in our family," and develop your own family traditions and rituals. And give your children the gift of memories by telling and retelling the special stories of your family's history—stories that make your family unique.

Remember, too, that through your family your children will learn that they belong to a much larger family, the family of humankind. And since their contributions to that family will help determine "the future of the people," your job as a parent may very well be the most important job in the world.

Chapter 6

HOME ACTIVITIES

- Hold a character talk with your child or children about alcohol, tobacco, and other drugs, keeping in mind their age(s) when you plan what to cover. Complete the guidesheet on page 220.
- Plan ways that you can share family stories and memories with your children. Fill in the guidesheet on page 221.
- Remember to take care of the caregiver, and complete the chart on page 195.

A child is a person who is going to carry on what you have started.

He is going to sit where you are sitting, and when you are gone,

Attend to those things which you think are important.

You may adopt all the policies you please, but how they are carried out depends on him.

He will assume control of your cities, states , and nations.

He is going to move in and take over your churches, schools, universities, and corporations.

All your books are going to be judged, praised, or condemned by him.

The fate of humanity is in his hands.

—Abraham Lincoln

The Job of My Life

Sometimes I wonder what to say
To make it better, to make it okay.
Sometimes I wonder just what to do,
Where to take a stand,
And how to help them through
Through the tough times and the glad times
The time we share as a family.
It's not long
The time we have together
Together as a family.
Active Parenting
The most important job in my life.
Active Parenting
Helped me do the job of my life.

And so I'm giving it all I can.
I'm a special part of a special plan.
And joy is growing within my heart
For my precious child as we make this start.
Active Parenting
The most important job in my life.
Active Parenting
Helped me do the job of my life.
Long ago, we didn't know
What challenges lay ahead
But now the joy is real,
And it's such a different feel
To love this child with my eyes opened wide.
Learning more each day
About the Active Parenting way
Active Parenting
The most important job in my life.
Active Parenting
Helped me do the job of my life.

—Michael H. Popkin

Active
PARENTING™
Now

Worksheets

Use these worksheets to reinforce the skills taught in this guide.
See the Home Activities at the end of each chapter for
a schedule and instructions for use.

Goals for Active Parenting

One thing I want to remember from the first video is:

One thing I want to learn from this program is:

Session 6

List three things that you have learned during this program:

1. _____

2. _____

3. _____

Do you feel that you've grown as a parent as a result of this program? If so, how?

_____

_____

_____

In what ways do you think the things you've learned have helped:

you? _____

_____

your child or children? _____

_____

your family? _____

_____

This worksheet refers to the 6-week Active Parenting Now *discussion program. If you are using this Parent's Guide independently and are interested in participating in a discussion group, check out the Parent tab at our website for a group being held near you.*

194

www.activeparenting.com

Taking Care of the Caregiver

Each week, record the things you do to take care of the caregiver—yourself—and check the categories that apply for each activity. You do not have to cover each category every week, but try to touch on each area at least once over the six-week period. For ideas and tips, see page 32-34.

Week		Keeping your body healthy	Contact w/ other adults	Clear your mind	Getting organized
1					
2					
3					
4					
5					
6					

The Method of Choice Activity

Choices I can give my child this week:

Child's name:

Choice Given:

How did it go?

Child's name:

Choice Given:

How did it go?

Child's name:

Choice Given:

How did it go?

Child's name:

Choice Given:

How did it go?

Family Enrichment Activity

Taking Time for Fun

Remember when . . .

Remember something fun you enjoyed doing as a child with one of your parents. Close your eyes for a moment and visualize the pleasant experience.

What was the fun activity you and your parent shared? _____

_____

How did you feel about your parent at that moment? _____

_____

How did you feel about yourself? _____

_____

Have a family meeting to decide how you will take time for fun within the next week. Record what you decide. _____

_____

_____

Progress Chart

As you take time for fun with each of your children, record the experience below:

Child's name _____ What did you do? _____

_____

How did it go? _____

_____

Child's name _____ What did you do? _____

_____

How did it go? _____

_____

Child's name _____ What did you do? _____

_____

How did it go? _____

_____

Communication Blocks Activity

We all use communication blocks at one time or another. Or, as one parent put it, "My skill is such that I can use three or four of these blocks at one time!" To catch ourselves before we block communication, it helps to know what our individual pitfalls are.

Think about the communication blocks you tend to use most often. Write them under "block" below. Then indicate the situations that usually bring them out, and what you see as your intention for using each block.

Situation	Block	Intention
Example: *Son didn't get the part in the school play.*	*Distracting*	*To make him feel better so I'd feel better.*
	Commanding	
	Sarcasm	
	Being judgmental	

Active Listening Activity

 Circle   feeling words   ⌈bracket⌉   alternatives and consequences

<u>Underline</u>   connecting feelings to content   "follow-up"   when mom follows up
                                                    (write in margin)

Ramon: I don't believe it!

Sandra: You don't believe what?

Ramon: Mrs. Hickman. I was sitting there minding my own business while Denise and Mark were passing notes back and forth and because I was between them they kept giving them to me to pass and then Mrs. Hickman turns around and sees me passing this note to Denise… only it wasn't from me, it was from Mark. But Mrs. Hickman thought it was from me and gave me extra homework because I "apparently have so much time on my hands that I don't know what to do." It isn't fair!

Sandra: You sure sound angry.

Ramon: Yes! Wouldn't you?! I mean it wasn't even my note!

Sandra: And yet you're the one who got in trouble. I can see why you'd be upset.

Ramon: And then, Denise and Mark didn't say a word. They just sat there and giggled.

Sandra: You must have been furious about that.

Ramon: Yeah! They started it, and then let me take all the blame!

Sandra: And of course all Mrs. Hickman saw was you passing the note.

        I guess you were a little embarrassed too, when Mrs. Hickman disciplined you in front of the whole class.

Ramon: Yeah. But the other kids saw what was going on, so it wasn't that bad. But now I have all this homework to do. It's not fair. I'm not going to do it.

Sandra: That's one thing you could do. What would happen if you don't do it?

Ramon: I guess Mrs. Hickman'd give me an "F" to average in with my grades.

Sandra: Ouch! That could really hurt, especially after all the hard work you've put in this year. What else could you do?

Ramon: I could tell her what really happened?

Sandra: Yes, you could. What do you think would happen then?

Ramon: Well…the other kids would probably call me a tattletale, and Mrs. Hickman would just tell me I had no business passing notes, anyway… that I should have ignored them.

Sandra: What do you think about that?

Ramon: I guess it was pretty dumb. I mean I guess I knew that she doesn't allow passing notes and all, but Mom, I didn't want the other kids to think I'm not cool.

Sandra: I see. You were afraid they wouldn't like you if you followed Mrs. Hickman's rules about no passing notes. So you let them get you in trouble because you want them to like you.

Ramon: Yeah. Pretty dumb, wasn't it?

Sandra: Well…let's put it this way: It's only dumb if you keep doing it. It may be a mistake that you can learn something from.

• • • • • • •

Sandra: Oh, Ramon. I've been meaning to ask—How did that passing notes problem work out? Did you do the extra homework?

Ramon: Yeah. I didn't think an "F" would be too great.

Sandra: And how about Mark and Denise? Are they still trying to get you to pass notes in class?

Ramon: No way! I told them I didn't like what they did, and that the next time I was just going to just ignore them.

Sandra: Attaboy. I like the way you stood up for yourself. It's smart to not let people take advantage of you.

Responding to Feelings Video Practice

Scene	Child's Feeling	Parent's Response
Jenny and Li		
Matthew and Sherry		
Ben and Katy		
Alina and Carlos		
Angela and Sherry		
Ramon and Sandra		
Austin and Tim		

This worksheet refers to the 6-week Active Parenting Now *discussion program. If you are using this Parent's Guide independently and are interested in participating in a discussion group, check out the Parent tab at our website for a group being held near you.*
www.activeparenting.com

Active Communication Evaluation

After you've had a chance to practice your active communication skills with one of your children this week, fill out the following evaluation so that you can be sure to learn from the experience.

What was the situation or problem that you talked to your child about?_____

_____

_____

How did you approach your child? _____

_____

_____

List examples of the five steps of active communication you were able to use:

1. Listen actively _____

_____

2. Listen for feelings _____

_____

3. Connect feelings to content _____

_____

4. Look for alternatives and evaluate consequences _____

_____

5. Follow up _____

_____

How did your child respond to your efforts? _____

_____

What did you like about how you handled the process?_____

_____

What would you do differently next time? _____

_____

Who Owns the Problem Video Practice

Scene	Who Owns the Problem?	Why?
Katy and Ben (fighting)		
Sandra and Ramon (getting up)		
Sherry and Angela (interrupting)		
_____ _____ _____ (a problem in your family)		

This worksheet refers to the 6-week Active Parenting Now *discussion program. If you are using this Parent's Guide independently and are interested in participating in a discussion group, check out the Parent tab at our website for a group being held near you.*
www.activeparenting.com

Family Enrichment Activity

Bedtime Routines and I Love You's

Family Meeting: Determine a Bedtime Routine

Hold a family meeting to determine a bedtime routine for each child. Be sure to cover the following:

What time is lights out for each child?_____

_____

What is the routine? (i.e. bath, pajamas, brush teeth, read a story, etc.) _____

_____

What happens if the routine is broken? _____

_____

Expressing Love at Home

Recall a time when an adult in your life expressed love to you. Maybe it was a parent, a grandparent, another relative, or a teacher. Maybe the expression was through words, maybe through an action like a pat on the back.

Describe the experience: _____

_____

How did you feel? _____

_____

To help you remember to tell your child you love him or her, fill in the following chart:

Child	Your Expression	Your Child's Response

Polite Requests, "I" Messages, and Firm Directions

1. Pretend that your child has just talked to you disrepectfully. Please write an example of a polite request that you could give your child:

   Please speak to me in a nicer way.

2. Let's assume that your child continues to speak disprespectfully to you. Construct an "I" message that you could give your child:

   I have a problem with _____

   I feel _____

   because _____

   I would like (Will you please) _____

3. Let's assume that the "I" message was not effective. Construct a firm direction for your child:

   _____

Home Example

Write down a problem from your own family in which you own the problem. _____

_____

Now write an "I" message that you can use at home this week to solve the problem: _____

_____

When _____

I feel _____

because _____

I would like (Will you please) _____

Evaluation

How did your child respond to your "I" message? _____

_____

What did you like about the way you delivered the "I" message? _____

_____

How would you do it differently next time? _____

_____

Logical Consequences Video Practice

Scene	Guideline Violated	Possible Logical Consequences
1. Sherry *Matthew not getting up*		
2. Tim *Ben fighting*		
3. Sandra *Alina's music too loud*		
4. Sherry *Angela not eating her peas*		

This worksheet refers to the 6-week Active Parenting Now *discussion program. If you are using this Parent's Guide independently and are interested in participating in a discussion group, check out the Parent tab at our website for a group being held near you.*

www.activeparenting.com

Using Logical Consequences

Think of a problem you would like to solve using a logical consequence. (You may choose the same problem for which you constructed an "I" message on page 112 as a back-up in case the "I" message is not effective.)

Write in the space below one way that you might present the choices and consequences to your child during the discussion of the problem. _____

_____

_____

Meet with your child to discuss the problem, and use this logical consequence or one that you develop with the child.

Evaluation

What was your child's response to the discussion? _____

_____

_____

What was his response to the logical consequence? (Did he test you to see if you would follow through?) _____

_____

If the consequence isn't working, do you think you need to stick with it longer or change the consequence to something else? _____

_____

If the consequence isn't working, have you violated any of the guidelines for setting up logical consequences? (Check page 90.) _____

What do you like about the way you handled the use of logical consequences? _____

_____

What will you do differently next time? _____

_____

Family Meeting: Problem-Prevention Talk

Before having your talk...

What topic will you discuss?

_____

_____

What are some specific concerns or risks that you want to share your thoughts and feelings about?

_____

_____

_____

_____

After your talk...

What guidelines did your family decide upon?

_____

_____

_____

_____

_____

What logical consequences or incentives, if any, did you include?

_____

_____

_____

What went well during the meeting?

_____

_____

_____

What will you do differently next time?

_____

_____

How will you follow-up on the guidelines?

_____

_____

Family Enrichment Activity
Positive "I" Messages

Plan a positive "I" message, and then give it to one of your children this week.

I would like _____

I feel _____

Because _____

How about if I _____

Afterwards...

What did you like about how it went? _____

_____

_____

_____

_____

What will you do differently next time? _____

_____

_____

_____

_____

_____

Four Goals Activity

Fill in this Think-Feel-Do chart with an example of a conflict that you have had recently with one of your children. Write the child's behavior under Event #1, then record your thoughts, feelings, and action. Finally, how did your child respond to your action?

Event

1. Child's behavior:

   _____

   _____

   _____

2. Response to correction:

   _____

   _____

   _____

Do

_____

_____

_____

Think

_____

_____

_____

Feel

_____

_____

_____

Child's goal: _____

Child's negative approach: _____

Child's "pay-off," if any: _____

Four Goals Home Observation

Analyzing the Problem Activity

Fill in this Parent-Child cycle chart with an example of a conflict that you have had recently with one of your children. Then answer the questions below.

Think

2. _____

_____

PARENT

Do

1. Child's behavior:

_____

_____

CHILD

Think

5. _____

_____

Feel

3. _____

_____

4. Your correction

_____

_____

Feel

6. _____

_____

What was my child's goal? (See chart on page 111.) _____

_____

What was my child's negative response to this goal? _____

_____

Did I "pay off" this negative approach? If so, how? _____

_____

If you used the FLAC method to redirect him to a positive approach, how did you use each step?

Feelings   _____

Limits   _____

Alternatives _____

Consequences _____

Family Meeting: Active Problem Solving

Choose a problem that you would like to handle with your child using the active problem solving process. It may be the same one that you chose for the logical consequences exercise or a new one that requires more teamwork.

_____

_____

_____

After you hold a meeting...

How did each step go?

1. Identify the problem.

_____

2. Share thoughts and feelings and acknowledge your child's thoughts and feelings.

_____

_____

3. Brainstorm possible solutions and guidelines.

_____

_____

4. Choose a solution, including a logical consequence if needed.

_____

_____

5. Follow-up later

_____

_____

What positive results came out of your discussion?

_____

_____

What will you do differently next time to improve the process?

_____

_____

_____

Family Enrichment Activity

Teaching Skills

List the names of your children and what skill you have decided to teach each child:

Child's Name	Skill To Be Taught
1. _____	_____
2. _____	_____
3. _____	_____

After you teach the skill, use the seven steps as a checklist:

	Child	1	2	3
1. Did you motivate the child?		❏	❏	❏
2. Did you select a good time when you weren't rushed?		❏	❏	❏
3. Did you break the skill down into baby steps?		❏	❏	❏
4. Did you demonstrate how to do this job?		❏	❏	❏
5. Did you let him or her try?		❏	❏	❏
6. Did you encourage?		❏	❏	❏
7. Did you work or play together afterwards?		❏	❏	❏

What went well with each child?

1. _____

2. _____

3. _____

What might you do to improve the experience next time? _____

_____

_____

If you chose for your child to teach you something, how did it go? _____

_____

_____

Stimulating Independence

Think of things that you are now doing for your children that they could be doing for themselves. For example, making their beds, picking up their clothes, cleaning up after them. Make a list below:

1. picking up dirty laundry/putting away clean
2. putting away toys
3. picking up dishes
4. _____
5. _____
6. _____
7. _____
8. _____

Now, choose one of these to let each child do for him- or herself this week. Be sure to be encouraging as you turn this over to each child, and practice our encouragement skills as each child progresses.

Afterwards . . .

What did you like about how it went? _____

_____

_____

_____

What can you do to improve things next time?_____

_____

_____

_____

Building on Strengths Activity: The BANK Method

Use the four steps of the BANK Method to encourage your child's progress in learning a skill or value. What is the goal that you would like to set for your child?

_____

Baby steps.

Write down five baby steps that your child will need to complete on the way to achieving this goal:

1. _____

2. _____

3. _____

4. _____

5. _____

Acknowledge what your child already does well. Write down three steps that your child has already mastered or strengths that will help your child achieve the goal:

1. _____

2. _____

3. _____

Next, talk with your child about the goal and acknowledge these strengths in the conversation. How did the talk go?

_____

Did you get your child's agreement to work on the goal together? If not, how will you approach your child differently next time? _____

_____

If your child agreed to work on the goal, fill in the final two steps after working together:

Nudge your child to take the next step. How did you encourage your child to take the next step? How did it go and what might you do to improve this next time? _____

_____

Keep encouraging improvement and persistence (especially after backsliding) until the goal is met. What words or actions did you find that were encouraging to your child? _____

_____

Showing Confidence

Find ways to encourage your child by showing confidence in one or more of the four ways detailed on pages 156 and 157. Then complete the questions for for the method(s) you chose.

1. What **responsibility** did you give your child? _____

   _____

   How did he or she handle it? _____

   _____

   How can you improve the situation? _____

   _____

2. What did you **ask your child's advice** about? _____

   _____

   How did he or she respond? _____

   _____

3. When did you **avoid the temptation to take over** for your child? _____

   _____

   How did you encourage your child to stick with it? _____

   _____

   How did he or she respond? _____

   _____

4. When did you **show that you expected success or positive behavior?** _____

   _____

   How did he or she respond _____

   _____

   What did you do to follow up? _____

   _____

Valuing the Child

Find ways to show that you value your child for what she is, using one or more of the methods detailed on pages 160 and 161. Then complete the questions for for the method(s) you chose.

1. How did you **separate worth from accomplishments**? _____

   _____

   How did he or she respond? _____

   _____

   What would you do the same or different next time? _____

   _____

2. How did you **separate worth from mishbehavior**? _____

   _____

   How did he or she respond? _____

   _____

   What would you do the same or different next time? _____

   _____

3. How did you show that you **appreciate your child's uniqueness**? _____

   _____

   How did he or she respond? _____

   _____

   What would you do the same or different next time? _____

   _____

4. What special **words and actions** did you use to let your child know that you value him just for himself—unconditionally? _____

   _____

   How did he or she respond? _____

   _____

   What would you do the same or different next time? _____

   _____

Family Meeting: Character Talk

Courage

Have a character talk about courage with your family this week and answer the following questions.

Before the talk...

How will you introduce the topic? _____
_____
_____

What are some points that you want to be sure to make during the talk? _____
_____
_____

What are some open-ended questions that you can use to stimulate discussion? _____
_____
_____

What outside resources such as articles, a story or video will you use to help you be more persuasive? _____
_____

Do you plan to make a collage to reinforce the character quality? If so, what kind of collage and where will you get the materials? _____
_____

After the talk...

What were some things that you liked about how the talk went? _____
_____

How did you listen with empathy as you discussed the topic together? _____
_____

What will you do differently next time to make it better? _____
_____

Family Enrichment Activity

Letter of Encouragement

Remember when . . .

Recall a time when one of your parents said or did something that you found encouraging when you were a child. Take a moment to visualize the experience and to rekindle the positive feeling it provided.

What did your parent do or say? _____

_____

How did you feel? _____

_____

Now, try to find a letter or note that you found encouraging . . . from your parents or someone else.

What encouraged you about it? _____

_____

Use this space to write a rough draft of a letter of encouragement to each of your children. Then copy the letter onto stationery or other paper before placing it where your child will find it—or mailing it!

_____

_____

_____

_____

_____

_____

_____

_____

_____

_____

_____

_____

Family Meeting: Character Talk
Alcohol, Tobacco, and Other Drugs

Have a character talk about tobacco, alcohol and other drugs with your family this week and answer the following questions.

Before the talk...

How will you introduce the topic? _____

_____

_____

What are some points that you want to be sure to make during the talk? _____

_____

_____

_____

What are some open-ended questions that you can use to stimulate discussion? _____

_____

_____

_____

What outside resources such as articles, a story or video will you use to help you be more persuasive? _____

_____

_____

After the talk...

What were some things that you liked about how the talk went? _____

_____

_____

How did you listen with empathy as you discussed the topic together? _____

_____

What will you do differently next time to make it better? _____

_____

_____

Family Enrichment Activity

In Our Family

Find a time to talk with your children about your family's history. You might include stories of how you came to this country or area, anecdotes about colorful family members, any special achievements and ways that you might honor their memories. Afterwards, answer these questions:

What special stories did you share? _____

_____

_____

_____

_____

_____

_____

_____

How did your children respond? _____

_____

_____

_____

Did you record the experience by video or other means? _____

_____

_____

_____

What will you do to improve the experience next time? _____

_____

_____

_____

10 Roles Parents Can Play in Preventing Problems with Drugs, Sexuality, and Violence

The Office of Substance Abuse Prevention (OSAP) suggests these 10 roles that parents can play in the prevention of drug use.

1. **Parents as role models.**
   Be a positive role model. Children learn best by example.

2. **Parents as educators and information resources.**
   Be informed about drugs, sexuality, and violence and talk with your child.

3. **Parents as policy makers and rule setters.**
   Make rules and enforce them. For example, "No use of illegal drugs by anyone in the family, and no use of alcohol or nicotine by anyone under the legal age."

4. **Parents as stimulators.**
   Encourage your child to take part in hobbies, school activities and sports. Get involved; plan fun family activities.

5. **Parents as consultants and educators on peer pressure.**
   "Just say no" is easier said than done. Teach your child to resist peer pressure without feeling foolish.

6. **Parents as monitors and supervisors.**
   Set and enforce curfews; know where your children are.

7. **Parents as collaborators with other parents.**
   Join with other parents to gain support and new ideas. There's strength in numbers.

8. **Parents as identifiers and confronters.**
   Know how to identify drug use and other problems and confront your child when necessary.

9. **Parents as managers of children's health.**
   Don't delay—seek medical help if you suspect your child is engaged in unhealthy behavior. Trust your instincts!

10. **Parents as managers of their own feelings.**
    Don't blow up; don't give up. You're not guilty.

This list is available as a large, color poster.
Contact Active Parenting Publishers for information.